T0121348

This book will be an important resource for those with a life-threatening condition and for the people that care for them. Dr. Penny's love and compassion is reflected through every word written in *"Healing Hope for Grief and Bereavement"* and I admire how she has given from the depth of her heart and tried her best to bring comfort and hope in such a time as in death and dying. *I highly recommend this creative work* toall who face the challenges of personal grief or providing quality care at life's final moments to loved ones or in their professions.

Gregory C. Townsend
Former Administrator, Birmingham Area Hospice

Dr. Penny Njoroge, who I lovingly refer to as Dr. Penny, has written an astounding masterpiece that teaches individuals how to use spirituality to cope with grief. Dr. Penny's thoughtful insight and sensitivity is exhibited throughout this work. Anyone facing a grieving situation would do well to read this guiding manual. This classic is a must read for all humans because we will face a grieving period at some time in our lifetime as a result of a death of a loved one or for many other diverse challenges . Congratulations Dr. Penny on a job well done. *You have definitely made grieving a little easier to cope with!!!!!!*

Dr. Charles Fields
President, Fields & Associates, Inc.

Dr. Penny Njoroge has been a leader among leaders in the American Pain Foundation Network for several years. As the State Leader for Alabama, Dr. Penny is part of a national grassroots advocacy effort working to raise awareness about the hidden epidemic of the under-treatment of pain and promoting positive pain policy and practice. She works tirelessly to shed light on the darkness of damaging misconceptions, speaks passionately for those who are without a voice and skillfully works with others to remove barriers to appropriate pain care. In her book *"Healing Hope For Your Grief and Bereavement"*, she brings her wealth of experience, compassion and passion that will inspire readers to embrace grief and healing with the same ways she has been a beacon of inspiration for others working to improve pain care. We applaud the inclusion of a chapter on pain care as it provides valuable information and powerful stories from a truly cross-cultural perspective. Out of her own personal experience with chronic pain, Dr. Penny passionately highlights and voices the deep impact of grief that chronic pain brings to millions who suffer silently in hiding for fear of being ridiculed and seen as weaklings when they acknowledge it and seek help. Her words give a vivid picture of the tragic impact of the lack of pain care has for individuals, families, friends and communities. As is true throughout her book, Dr. Penny weaves messages of hope and inspiration for all of us to urgently transform our compassion into action to improve the lives of others. *This is definitely a book worth reading and recommending to family and friends.*

Mary Bennett, MFA
Director of Grassroots Advocacy
American Pain Foundation

As a Registered Nurse, I often encounter the terminally ill, the dying and grieving families in my work. Reading through this book has both challenged and helped me. Not only is the title capturing but the book contents are very enticing for everyone both as a professional helping others through such experiences or for those personally undergoing grief for one reason or another. Dr. Penny is not only humble and visionary, but is also encouraging, intelligent, uplifting and very articulate in her writing. She effectively teaches in her book what and when to say in such circumstances and comes out as a very compassionate and caring person to everyone reading this book. Dr. Penny has been honored numerous times and received many distinguished awards including a ***Head of State Commendation (HSC)*** from the President of The Republic of Kenya for her work in the community, in her counseling the grieving, the broken hearted and those challenged by all kinds of problems. In a very soft spoken approach, she has comforted and reassured numerous people undergoing life shattering experiences and is well known in the community for reaching out to others in crisis situations. She is also very effective and passionate in empowering and motivating people in helpless\hopeless circumstances to rise up from the ashes of their pain and learn to live beyond their tragedies. ***THIS BOOK IS A MUST READ for everyone.***

Mary Mathangani, RN, CN
Trinity Hospital, Birmingham, Al

To know Dr. Penny Njoroge means having a kindred relationship with someone who speaks directly from the heart. She expresses genuine concern for others, meets everyone with a smile and greets you with warmth and acceptance. She has a deeply nurturing spirit and her words are sincere and encouraging. She is good at empowering others to survive painful situations to become living testimonies of God's healing hope and grace.

Dr. Penny embodies a spirit of giving back and reaching out to those in need. Although her life requires her to comfort those who are bereaved, she is talented and naturally gifted in her ministry of HOPE as she exemplifies a mission to aid, support and nurture those in pain and struggle.

She is well aware of the ingredients essential to overcome grief by the continuous counsel and ministry from the word of God. This book, ***Healing Hope for Your Grief & Bereavement,*** is a true and down to earth testament of her daily work and walk through life. Dr. Penny is constantly working in the vineyard of the Lord by helping others to overcome that which we must all face at one point or another as we journey through life.

Dr. Penny is well informed and knowledgeable on the matters of grief and bereavement from her professional, practical and daily walk with the terminally ill, the dying and those left behind to mourn and grieve their loved ones. She is very caring, compassionate and tender with others at such moments. Dr. Penny has left lasting impressions on many people's lives through her ministry wherever she has worked, and is highly respected by everyone both at work and in our community at large. She has received a lot of honors and recognition for her highly effective ministry. ***I HIGHLY RECOMMEND THIS BOOK TO EVERYONE.***

Sandra Owens
Risk Management Coordinator
St. Vincent's East Hospital

HEALING HOPE
FOR YOUR GRIEF
& BEREAVEMENT

Dr. Penny Wanjiru Njoroge

WestBow
PRESS
A DIVISION OF THOMAS NELSON

Copyright © 2010 Dr. Penny Wanjiru Njoroge

All rights reserved. No part of this book may be used or reproduced by
any means, graphic, electronic, or mechanical, including photocopying,
recording, taping or by any information storage retrieval system
without the written permission of the publisher except in the case
of brief quotations embodied in critical articles and reviews.

WestBow Press books may be ordered through booksellers or by contacting:

WestBow Press
A Division of Thomas Nelson
1663 Liberty Drive
Bloomington, IN 47403
www.westbowpress.com
1-(866) 928-1240

Because of the dynamic nature of the Internet, any Web addresses or
links contained in this book may have changed since publication and
may no longer be valid. The views expressed in this work are solely those
of the author and do not necessarily reflect the views of the publisher,
and the publisher hereby disclaims any responsibility for them.

ISBN: 978-1-4497-0450-6 (sc)
ISBN: 978-1-4497-0621-0 (e)

Library of Congress Control Number: 2010935751

Printed in the United States of America

WestBow Press rev. date: 9/10/2010

I would like to dedicate this book to a few people who God specifically put in my life for a very divine and humbling purpose for my spiritual life and walk.

I am for ever grateful for my father Lawrence and mother Miriam who have both left this life and taken their eternal resting places in heaven. It was my parents who constantly reminded me throughout their presence in my life that "Quitting was not an option" and despite the adversities I will face in my journey, God's divine plans and destiny for my life would never change or fail, if I remained focused and connected with Him. It is their loving soft voices of encouragement that have kept me going when I felt like quitting as the Master Potter melted and molded me into the person I am today. I will always honor their names and thank God for their permanent prints on my life.

The best and priceless gifts in my life are my six children, each of who is a unique and precious jewel. Paul, Lawrence, Stella, Evelyn, Eric and Mary have all stood faithfully and in steadfast love and care during the most trying seasons as I traveled through my personal valleys of both grief and bereavement. Each of them fully aware of, not only my strengths but my worst weaknesses, have given me devoted love and support as I faced my giants in tears and frustrations and constantly reminded me that with God's promised help, I had the capacity to make it in life. They stood by me at the worst moment of my life as I battled a painful divorce after 30 years of marriage. At my most vulnerable moments when all I prayed for was to die, they stuck it out with me and gave me no other choice but to survive and celebrate their children, my grandchildren. I am humbled and grateful because were it not for them, I would never have lived long enough to see the greatest miracles in my life. I owe the completion of this book to them because they have been the best cheerleaders I would have prayed for in moments when I wanted to shelve the manuscript and forget all about it. I passionately dedicate this book to each of them.

Finally, I dedicate this book to my most beautiful grandchildren Ayanna, Shayna, Ava, Jonathan and the precious one who should be joining our family in a couple of months. The birth of each of them has heralded a new beginning for me and a renewed meaning for life. They are each a silver lining in my challenging moments and for them I bless God for my future generations. I dedicate this book to them and those who come into my life hereafter. For all the above and my many friends, I thank God for their undying support.

Contents

FOREWORD

First and foremost, I give thanks to God our almighty Father for His goodness and love. He has been my provider and my protector. I would not be where I am today, if I had not been strong in my faith. God's covering has helped me to weather the *storm*! It would have been a blessing to me and made some of my own struggles easier to deal with if I had Dr. Penny's words to guide me, as well as, my family. Her book, *Healing Hope for Grief and Bereavement*, provides encouraging words and details examples of how to first acknowledge what is or has happened to you and how best to deal with it. I have read it and it is powerful and encouraging!

I am 45 years old and have experienced loss at various levels: both parents, grandparents, best friends, and a sister-in-law. The most difficult for me was growing up without my parents. Both of my parents died a tragic death at such a young age. I am the oldest of four children and was just shy of 5 years old when they died. I remember going to their funerals, the burial, and even asking my grandmother where my mom was and when she was coming back home. I recall her vividly saying," your mom is in heaven." At such a young age, I really did not understand why she was not coming home. There were many nights I cried for my mom and dad. I just could not understand why they were gone and why my cousins and friends had their parents and I did not.

My grandparents were God fearing people and did a great job taking care of me and my three siblings. As I look back, if I had to choose three things that helped me heal over the years, I would say it was God, being able to forgive, and my grandparent's open and honest conversations about my parents and life in general. Dr. Penny also talks about open and honest conversations in her book. Having the strength to talk about what hurts you the most is part of the healing process. The worst thing that you can do is not acknowledge that you are grieving and not be willing to talk about how you feel. I think of my parents everyday and often find myself starring at the family photo taken the Christmas before their death. I often wonder how and if my life would have been different if they had lived. Life has been great and I have been blessed with a wonderful family, very close friends, and a very successful career. I married my high school sweetheart and have two beautiful children. In the midst of it all, every child and adult longs for their mother and father. I still do, but in a healthy and spiritual way.

I have experienced many other facets of loss and grief that are too many to detail. If you are reading the foreword of this book, you have taken the first step in acknowledging that either you personally or someone you know needs spiritually guided steps to grief recovery and bereavement. I wish you much success and stress that you keep the Word of God in your heart and allow Him to guide your steps.

Peace and Blessings,

Dr. Carol Jefferson Ratcliffe, RN, CNOR, FACHE

Introduction

Life itself is mystifying, but one thing that is certain is that we all will experience loss. When this occurs, it takes on a new meaning for each of us. ***Healing Hope for Grief and Bereavement*** takes us through life's journey that we all will face or have the potential to face at some point in our lives. It requires faith, hope, support, and inner strength to overcome and deal with death, separation, or even divorce. What may be a simple adjustment for one person may take a lifetime of transition for another. You simply need to understand that this is o.k. Men and women, children, teenagers, and people with different ethnic backgrounds respond differently in their adaptation to loss and grief and how they heal.

Through ***Healing Hope for Grief and Bereavement.*** Dr. Penny gives real life examples, transcending through the stages and processes of grief and types of loss, with guidance on how to heal the hurt and pain and your soul. Self preservation is an important component to your success along the continuum of healing. Through life and this book, Dr. Penny also helps you to learn that it is acceptable to cry, to talk about how you feel, and to seek the help of a medical professional. The Word of God resonates throughout this book as a constant reminder that you are never alone. Seek His help and you shall find solace in His Word. Life is full of challenges and many are difficult to overcome. When you take the initial step to help yourself or allow someone else to help you, you are well on your way! Remember, that God loves you and He will grant you a new beginning.

The book is well written with many illustrations from different aspects of life and I would recommend it for everyone. If you have not yet experienced grief and loss it will give you some ideas on how to be an effective support for others in their moments of grief and bereavement. I also prepares you for that inevitable day or season when we must each travel through that valley of grief, pain and tribulation for one reason or another. Dr. Penny also helps you understand why people respond the way they do in their different moments of struggle and brokenness.

1

The Impact of Death, Dying, & Grief

As I sit and reflect on this topic, it quietly dawns on me that whoever walks through life must inevitably experience a moment of grief for one reason or another. And this goes for all the living creatures of the earth. From the huge elephants to the minute insects like the ants etc. In the African jungles, the huge elephants have been known to linger around a dead mate, offspring or parent for days, refusing to move, overcome with grief, loss and sadness, until the shock subsides and a sense of acceptance takes over.

Children and adults alike, have been know to grieve the loss of a beloved pet so painfully as if a fellow human being had passed away. Wherever there has been some form of relationship and friendship; separation by death, divorce or other will inevitably cause pain, grief and trauma especially if not adequately dealt with.

The pain of loosing to death a parent, a child, a spouse/ partner, a sibling or close friend, colleague or neighbor has a tendency of shaking up the very roots of our lives, turbulently.

The extent of the grief will depend on the relationship that existed with the deceased.

In many cultures, death is not an easy topic of discussion. Across the universe, people avoid talking about death almost as if you can avoid it by not talking or thinking about it. Or as if when you talk about it you call or draw it upon yourself or those that we love. The reality is that either way, every human being has a destiny with death.

The bible tells us that there is a time and a place for everything in life. A time to be born and a time to die. Under the same token, a time to celebrate the birth of a new baby into our lives and families but inevitably for this same baby there will be a time to mourn or grieve for their departure out of our lives and back to their creator God. I say this as a believer, knowing that through the death of Jesus Christ on the cross, God made a provision for us to go back home for which we were all made. Yes, into an endless and timeless eternity with him, never to grieve, loose our loved ones again. Never to feel the brokenness, helplessness, hopelessness etc that accompany us through grief and bereavement. In the meantime, the Lord promises to heal the broken hearted and bind their wounds (Psalm 147:3). Like David in his many crossroads of grief and heartache despite being "A man after God's own Heart", we need to ask God "May your gracious spirit lead me forward on a firm footing" as I travel through this grief (Psalm 143:10b)"

The flesh and blood in us will mourn and grieve but will also be sustained by the hope of seeing our beloved departed brothers in their new and glorified forms when I too join them after my death, to be mourned by those I leave behind.

Grief is therefore an unavoidable circle into which we must some day enter. I have lost many friends in life, but the death of my two younger brothers 14 and three years ago followed by both of my parents one after the other within 4 months gave death, dying and grief a very personal meaning. It has touched my life directly and personally. My work as a hospice/hospital chaplain has also exposed me to this monster as a minister, counselor and pastoral support on a full time basis. The truth is that one can never get used or comfortable with death, no matter how often you see or experience it daily. The finality and separation through death is an experience like no other.

As we deal with any and all kinds of losses, God may feel so far away. We might even wonder in our brokenness if God really understands or cares about our sorrow. And if so, we wonder why we have to part with all those we love. But in Isaiah 53:3-6 we read that He (Jesus) was a man of sorrows, rejected and despised, acquainted with bitterest grief. He has borne our grief and carried our sorrow. By His stripes we are healed.

Dealing with grief is almost like going through deep and turbulent waters that threaten to swallow you. It may also feel like going through intensely hot fires that are almost consuming you. Yet in Isaiah 43:1-5 God promises his protection and covering for our safety. While we may never forget or fully recover from our losses, grief or bereavement, things will gradually get better and bearable as time goes by. But how and at what pace this happens is unique to every person. There is therefore no A-Z method of grief and recovery set on hard stone. We must allow ourselves to process our grief in our own individual ways.

2

Experiencing the Death of a Loved One

There are many taboo subjects in many cultures across the universe, but death is yet the most sad or sacred experience in life. As much as we know everyone born of woman has a definite destiny with death, death and dying have from generation to generation, been cloaked in silence and mystery and few people ever want to address this topic until forced to do so by circumstances. Unfortunately, death is no respecter of persons and will catch up with the strong and the feeble, the old, the young and the unborn, the rich and the poor and makes its visits and harvest in all corners of the earth.

For believers, death is a brief separation from those that we love and cherish, but not the end. In John 11 verses 25-26 Jesus said "I am the resurrection and the life, those who believe in me, even though they die like everyone else, will live again. They are given eternal life for believing in me and will never perish." A human being has three dimensions – body, spirit and soul (mind, will and emotions). Paul says in 2 Corinthians 5:8 "Yes we are fully confident, and we would rather be away from these bodies, for then we will be at home with the Lord".

When someone's life is over in this world, the mortal body perishes. If they believed in Jesus Christ, though they are physically dead, they will live for ever in the spirit and also in our memories. Paul reminds us that "*To be absent from this body is to be present with the Lord*". For the initial grieving period, we will inevitably undergo emotional pain and grief. The intensity of our grief will vary from person to person; dependent on the relationship we had with the person who has passed away, their age and sometimes how they died. However, we gradually start adjusting to their absence from our lives, making small steps back and forth in our healing process. We begin to deal with their memories, retaining the good memories that will help you continue as best as is humanly possible, with your life. As much as is possible, try to discard those memories that bring back heartache from your past and may hinder your progress now or in the future. Unfortunately, you may have some unfinished issues that you might have to deal with before they can go away. Fond memories will help in your healing, especially any good plans you might have worked on together with your departed loved ones, e.g. with a spouse, with your parent(s), your siblings, your child or even a friend. At times, it might help to ask yourself, "How would (your loved one) want me to do with my life in their absence?" I doubt if anyone would want any of their surviving family to grieve for ever. Some have even said they would want the best for those surviving them, especially where long periods of major illnesses have preceded a death. The dying person has often been heard praying and hoping that their families and caregivers would learn to take care of themselves, do the things they have missed on like self grooming, going on a deserved holiday, going to church or visiting families near and far. Some have wished them just time to rest and enjoy themselves after all the care they have accorded them.

As believers, the Holy Bible reminds us in Jeremiah 1:5 "Before you were born I set you apart and appointed you s my spokesperson to the world". David also said that our days are numbered and God **_alone_** knows our end from the beginning. Whatever mode of death and time catches up with us might surprise us and our loved ones; but no death ever surprises our God and creator, whether early or late in life. Knowing that after death we will either go to heaven or hell might bring some kind of fear in people when death approaches us or our loved ones. But the good news is that Jesus Christ died on the cross to redeem each of us, paying in full the cost of our sins with his own cleansing blood, for us to have life and have it more abundantly, free from sin and death. In doing so, He secured an eternal life for all who believe in Him.

As a hospice/hospital chaplain, I have been blessed in experiencing the death of believers who knew fully well "where they were headed". While like everyone else they would be concerned with their survivor's" fate, more often than not, they die in peace. They die in great anticipation even in the midst of painful terminal illnesses, yearning and hungry for a better land and life where they will be free from their pain, sorrow and tears that was a part of their living for few or many years. Many are even able to boldly tell you what they are looking for in their next "home", like my own late mother who kept telling us that she could barely wait to get there and sing for the Lamb of God for ever. Some have actually been heard saying they are ready to go and that they see angels beckoning them. Others say they see their long gone parents, siblings or children. As much as they are concerned for those they will be leaving behind, they see death as an open door into a better and everlasting life.

On the contrary, I have seen some people on their dying bed suddenly gripped by great fear as they experience their bodies gradually declining and something tells them time is running out for them. Being critically ill, they suddenly face the reality of their eminent death and departure from this life. On several occasions, I have had the humbling experience of leading some to Christ at the last hour while they were scared and not sure that God would accept them because of the life they have led. To them death becomes a feared threat because of their uncertain future. For some to whom salvation has been offered and rejected in the past, they suddenly realize that a permanent and final transition is about to take place and ask how they can receive Christ's forgiveness and if God would still give them a chance. Some have changed their eternal home at the last hour while some have sadly missed out when death struck them suddenly or they lost their minds before deciding. But God in His infinite love stands watching and waiting till our last breath wanting to give us an eternity with him. He patiently waits to give everyone a chance to accept His gift of eternal life. Romans 6:23 says "For the wages of sin is death; but the free gift of God is eternal life through Christ Jesus our Lord".

It is a very comforting thing to know that our departed loved one walked with the Lord to the end, which also gives us a hope and desire to see them again in the heavenly home. Sadness and grief will still be there, but eased by that hope. Perhaps we too owe the same hope and gift to our own families and friends after we die like everyone else will.

Yes, death is definitely messy, painful and unbearable. It causes us to feel as if we are separated or alienated from God. It may also challenge our beliefs and bring a crisis in our faith. But for believers, there is something greater, beautiful and profound beyond pain and loss. There is HOPE. The Lord has promised to prepare a place in heaven above. This is a home where we will always be with him and those that we love dearly.

"I'm pressing on the upward way, new heights I'm gaining every day

Still praying as I'm onward bound, lord plant my feet on higher ground."

Philippians 4:14 challenges us to keep pressing on towards the prize of eternal life.

One of the hardest places and moments in life can be standing beside the bed either at home, hospital or wherever else, witnessing the death of a loved one. Even the thought of such a moment is itself very scary for many people, but it happens often. I have been called to be with families as the doctors turn off life support machines and other gadgets to let somebody's loved one pass on from this life to another in death. It may be from a terminal illness or after a fatal accident. This is a traumatic experience which only those who have experienced it can understand. The reality is that even when one has been sick for a long time and death was expected, it is always very difficult to let go. When families are asked by the doctors to give consent for them to turn off any life support, many are left with the guilt of letting go of their loved ones. This will be part of their healing needs in their grieving process.

Keeping a vigil when a loved one is dying is a very sacred experience when family members may gather to say their goodbyes and provide care to their loved one. All care at this point is now focused on keeping the patient as comfortable as possible, rather than treating medical conditions. But the thought of being present when someone is dying or taking their very last breath is scary to many people. Learning to recognize the signs of imminent death, knowing how to talk to the dying person, and knowing what to do after death occurs will help alleviate your fears and allow you to stay with your loved one through the closing of the circle of life and death. He/she may be communicating to the last minute while others are in a comma. It is said that even when they are in a comma and unresponsive, the last sense to go is hearing. We are therefore encouraged to say our goodbyes and assure them of our love now and always.

If possible and while your loved one is still able to hear and communicate with you, it is important to discuss any unfinished business, get them to tell you their personal wishes, especially, for after they are gone out of this life. It would be important to write down

some of these things especially where some family members live far away and may need to know the dying persons wishes and plans for her survivors. A living will outlining what they would like done or not done for them if they became critically ill and unable to communicate is very important. The presence of such instructions will alleviate misunderstandings between those left behind. It will also ensure that nothing is done to them in their dying moment that they did not want like codes and other very aggressive measures when the circumstances clearly indicate that they are not getting better. The absence of such written instructions leaves no choice but for the medical personnel to do whatever measures they deem necessary to keep the patient alive until their bodies give up. The worst thing is that it places traumatic and unpleasant responsibility on one's family at such times, putting them through experiences that might haunt them for the rest of their lives.

A written will instructing those who survive you on how your estate should be settled is of paramount importance. This too will take away the unnecessary misunderstandings among family members, which may unnecessarily affect their relations for many years to come. Aware that we all have a date with death, it is therefore important that as much as we can, we keep our "house" in order, especially if one has a family for whom we would like to leave a lasting legacy.

It is ironic that after all the struggles and efforts we undergo trying to make a name, wealth and so forth, the most important things are the "Precious Memories" that we leave behind to be passed down from one generation to another long after we are gone out of this life.

This may be a very appropriate time to share some five important things before it is too late.

> *"Please forgive me", "I forgive you", "Thank*
> *you", "I love you" and "Goodbye"*
> *(Ira Byrock – 1998)*

Death

I know little of what is on the other side of death, but
I do know one thing, I know my Master is there, and that
is enough"

A few months or years after we die, people may never remember how well we dressed, the kind of cars we drove or the earthly mansions we lived in. They will mostly remember the lasting impressions and impact we had on their lives – good or bad. It is a good time to repair our relationships – forgive and reconcile with each other. We need to pass on our blessings and personal stories. It would be nice to have lived a life that was like an arrow pointing them to Christ and the hope of glory, because there would be an anticipation of being reunited again.

3

WHAT IS GRIEF?

Grief is like a sudden, unexpected and unplanned journey with no road map or time to pack or psychologically prepare oneself. It is like suddenly having to jump out of a plane in a parachute without any warning. You have no idea where or how you will land and what life will be like if you survive and when you land wherever. It involves emotions, feelings and often times diverse physical reactions or symptoms. Grief takes you through unexpected places and uncharted territories, with feelings of never knowing what to expect at any given time. It is a multi-faceted response to loss. While grief is mostly viewed as an emotional response, it has other dimensions like physical, cognitive, behavioral, social and psychological issues. Grief is an emotionally wrenching experience filled with all kinds of vivid and contradictory feelings. Grief is therefore not just sadness, but many other things go with it. Grief is the feeling of reaching out to someone who has always been there, only to find when we desperately need them just once more, they are no longer there. It is however related to our self concept. Grief is often influenced by our attitudes and opinions, politics, religion and our philosophy of life. It is a stressful experience which can adversely affect one's health and life thereafter. Sometimes, many aspects of our background will affect or impact our grieving process like varied ethnic religious groups, each with their own rituals about death, different gender roles (male or female) may affect how we grieve. For example, most men may be reluctant to cry or show their emotions openly. Some people may want to visit the grave while others do not want to.

The first thing that is mostly thought of when the word "Grief" is mentioned anywhere is the loss to death of a loved one. Grief is a normal and natural response resulting in a conflicting mass of human emotion to any kind of loss that brings discomfort or major changes to one's life. There are many other un-acknowledged losses like divorce, broken relationships, loss of a new or long-held job, a major life changing terminal illness, relocation, retirement, diagnosis with a chronic illness, loss of a family home passed on from many generations, and many other kinds. It is more of a state of being than just emotions of sorrow, sadness and suffering. It also brings a deep sense of powerlessness, even hopelessness.

When grieving, one may even wish to skip the holiday gatherings. This is normal and okay. The sad thing is that we live in a world that has limited ability to talk openly and honestly about grief, resulting in isolation and loneliness for those grieving. Grief is almost always a taboo topic and we are mostly ill prepared and inadequately equipped to address it when death strikes. It is like a roller coaster of emotions. Unfortunately, we end up circulating lots of misinformation. By acting strong for our children, showing no feelings, we teach our children to do the same. In dealing with grief, there will be a wide variety of responses often influenced by people's personalities, family, culture, social habits and rules, spirituality, religious beliefs and practices, family traditions and protocol, step or extended families, separated/divorced families. Grief is not necessarily an enemy but also a friend that leads us into dealing with our loss and pain. However long the grieving process will take, it does get better and bearable gradually, allowing us to move on with life somehow. We often say "*It is in the valley of life that we learn the greatest lessons of life*". With life comes the long difficult and painful process of finding and developing life beyond loss. Experiencing the grief and loss of a loved one is traveling into a valley like no other. The reality is that there is a valley between every mountain. Valleys are those dark experiences that strengthen our minds, teach us the greatest lessons of faith, strength and patience. But the most important and needed thing is the lesson of **HOPE**. Hope that gradually the high and low of life will become less intense. But it may take years to get over the loss. Hope encourages us to lean on God and allow him to carry us through our sorrow when nothing else is working to soothe our pain and anguish of loss. Paul reminds us in 1 Thessalonians 4:13-14 "Not to be full of sorrow like people who have no hope. For if we believe that Jesus died and was raised to life again, we also believe that when Jesus comes, God will bring back with Jesus all the Christians who have died"

WHAT IS BEREAVEMENT?

Unlike Grief which covers many diverse losses, bereavement is experienced at the death and loss of a loved one. Even though bereavement is a normal part of life for everyone who has survived the death of a loved one, be it a parent, sibling, child, spouse/partner, close friend or colleague, it carries a certain amount of risk if adequate support is not made available or sought. Some of the risks may include breakup of marriages, especially after the loss of a child, personal faith and belief system may be challenged; some mental illnesses can also be traced to have been triggered by the loss of a loved one.

It is not unusual to see a grieving person who has been so totally dependent on the deceased loved one, that when death strikes they feel completely incapacitated and loose all meaning to their own lives. Some end up suicidal or self destructive. It was at such a time that David confessed loosing hope and feeling paralyzed with fear (psalm 143:4) "I am losing all hope; I am paralyzed with fear". Some people may be able to process their bereavement gradually alone, but others would do better by seeking help from professional bereavement counselors to promote and help with the healing process. It would also be helpful if possible, to go for Grief counseling support groups either professionally or peer-led.

4

Experiencing Grief and Bereavement

In many parts of the world, it is viewed as a weakness to express or expose your grief or bereavement. While both of these experiences may linger on for months or even years for some people, society will predominantly hurry you up to "get over it" and "move on with life" like everyone. It is not unusual to see someone bury a parent, a child, a spouse or other family members and return to work immediately and stoically stand up strong and bold while their broken hearts are secretly bleeding and hurting so bad. Unless dealt with properly and gradually, if grief is suppressed, it is likely to explode somewhere in the near or distant future most unexpectedly in many forms. Some of them as drastically as going into serious bouts of depression, feeling suicidal or literary crumbling down emotionally, spiritually or even morally to the extent of needing hospitalization for safety and recovery. When we focus on the major tragedies affecting humanity in every corner of the universe, we can say there are so many "Sudden Deaths" of freedom, safety and control (by Russell Friedman and John W. James of the Grief Recovery Institute)

Normal Reactions to Grief vs. Myths about Grief:

It is very important to keep in mind always that grieving is a process or a journey and not a final event. In different countries, cultures and traditions, death, dying, grief and end of life mattes are approached with great apprehension. We all know that everyone who has a day when they were born must have a day when they will die. It does not matter whether one is dead just a few days, weeks or months after conception or over a hundred years, but as in every other aspect of life, whatever has a beginning has a definite end. The Egyptian Kings and others, prepared enormous and expensive burial places in pyramids, acknowledging that as rich and famous as they were, they knew that some day in their future they would die and leave this life.

It is therefore ironical that most people will talk and joke about everything in life but are not at all comfortable with the subject of death and whatever goes with it. It is for this reason that most people die without a will on their estate or even a living will to guide others on what they would want done for them in case of a serious illness where they can no longer express their wishes. In most cases, people behave as if not talking about death will keep it at a distance from us. But the bible tells us that God knows our end from the very beginning. David also prays that God would help us to know and realize that our days in life are numbered.

The reality and truth is that grief is a very personal experience where nobody can quite tell you how to process it. Yet in some cultures and countries there are set patterns of grieving. In many places, there are things "To do" and "Not to do". My experience is that when people tell you to stop weeping or crying in your grieving process, it is because you make them uncomfortable and they do not know how to handle you. Unaware of what is going on, they do this to take care of themselves and their discomfort around you, not necessarily for the grieving person who is weeping or crying. If one feels tearful, it is only fair to allow them to do what helps them best. Most people feel that tears are a sign of weakness. However, the truth is that crying in your grief is a very normal process that helps relieve one's feelings. There is nothing shameful about it and people should be allowed to do what helps them most, including weeping. Let us remember too that "Jesus Wept" when he learnt that His friend Lazarus had died. (John 11:35) When a death takes place in the family, a lot of people will try to keep the children from everything that is going on around the death. This is a sad way of dealing with it, especially if the child had a relationship or interaction with the deceased. They too have reason to walk through the grieving process, since they will inevitably notice the absence of this person from the family or close friends. It is important to include the children, using appropriate language and explanations of what is going on. This raises the need to keep the children informed when there is a serious illness in the family that may eventually result in death so that the children too will not be taken by surprise. This lays some necessary stepping stones for the adults when death strikes and one has to explain to the children what happened to their parent, grand parent, sibling or any other member of the family who dies. This also facilitates for the children to grow up aware that people die and we need to be careful how we relate with others while still alive.

Once death has taken a loved one, people become anxious and tense around the grieving families, not knowing what to say to comfort them without hurting them. In the process, some people will totally avoid discussing a loss with the grieving persons. Unfortunately, this might leave them feeling very lonely and isolated in the midst of many people. On the contrary, grieving persons normally appreciate friends willing to share the good memories of the deceased person and even talk about the pain that loss and grief has brought to this family. As friends and family do this with the grieving people, you help break the element of grief (the big elephant in the room) instead of going round and round about it without attacking it.

In many cases, the grieving person is so very afraid of moving on with life. The fear that they will be seen or experienced as abandoning or forgetting the deceased loved one. But this is not so because love will last beyond grief through one's commitment to living fully. Perhaps the deceased person would actually rejoice at seeing the grieving person picking up their broken pieces and the family baton, move on a step at a time, and be able to carry on the legacy they both worked on together. Moving on may not be automatic or easy, but it is worth the effort. The uniqueness of grief also encourages us to be open to those wanting to support and companion us through the grieving and mourning process. We will therefore need to tell people what kind of help we need most. Teach others about your loss and they will support you more effectively.

The most common way offered to deal with our grief is to try to move away from grief and hope it will go away quickly, but unfortunately, the more you suppress it the harder it will be when finally it catches up with you and explodes at the wrong time and places. Instead, one should move towards the pain, experience it and allow yourself all the space and time you need to handle it appropriately. Grief is not a matter of the head but of the heart.

It is hard to tell when one has finally gotten over their grief; even though we constantly hear others tell us to "Get Over" with the grief and move on with life. We cannot say it often enough that this too will vary from person to person. However, there are some things that will let you know how well or badly you are doing with your grief. It is important to watch out on this so that if your grief is prolonged and intensifying instead of subsiding, you can seek professional help to carry you over the hardest points. Here are just a few indicators of how well you are processing your grief:

- Life begins to have increased meaning and hope again.

- Your eating and sleeping habits stabilize.

- You are able to enjoy life, relax, read or sing without guilt

- You have new reasons to look forward into the future.

- You feel comfortable renewing old relationships or establishing new ones in the community or in your working place.

- You find it easier to adjust to new changes in life.

- You experience new aspects of growth as you gradually move from your bereavement period, confident that you have had adequate time grieving

- You finally acknowledge and accept your new identity (widow/widower/orphan etc) seeing it as a part of life from now on

- You gradually realize that you can never get over your grief, but you become reconciled with it and live on as best as you can.

- You are comfortable expressing the pain of your grief and not suppressing it.

STAGES AND PROCESS OF GRIEF:

Dr. Elizabeth Kubler-Ross and others have labeled this as a "Grief Cycle". The stages will not fall in the same manner or sequence for everyone since we all grief differently. The way different people grieve is also dependent on the relationship between the deceased and the grieving person(s). It may also depend on the age, the circumstances of death and numerous other dynamics. The sad reality is that we may have expected the death especially after long periods of sickness or terminal illness, but, we are still ill prepared for grief. There five commonly experience stages of grief:

1. **Denial:**

At the point of receiving news of a death, or being present with the dying person and experiencing them taking their last breath one may be overwhelmed by a sense of total disbelief. One may even hope that this is just a dream which will soon pass away and the deceased will still be alive and hopefully getting better if they have been sick. This may be so when the deceased has been sick for long, recovered and bloomed for a few days and then suddenly passes away when everyone assumed they were on their way to full recovery. This is a point and place in life where the grieving person is unable to come to terms with what has just happened to change their lives for ever. Some may intentionally keep themselves too busy taking care of "stuff", even acting as if nothing has happened and often tell you that they are doing "just fine". This often happens in the case of a spouse death where the widow or widower feels the need to be strong, protective and available to their children. It can also happen in the case of an eldest sibling/ eldest child (the family caregiver) in the loss of another sibling or any of their parents. They too will be too busy taking care of things, comforting and being strong for the other siblings or the surviving parent. They may keep themselves too busy with the funeral and other arrangements, taking no time to process their own grieving and face their own loss. It is important to allow yourself to experience the pain and not try to escape it by staying too busy or taking medication to numb your pain. A period of shock and denial can last from hours to days to months. The more traumatic and unexpected the death, the longer the shock may last. Suppressing your grief will only delay the grieving process and intensify the feelings. While working through the grief is the best thing, unfortunately it is one of the hardest things in life.

I was such a person after the sudden tragic motor vehicle accident death of my younger brother who followed me and my best friend. He left behind five children, the youngest only three weeks old and a young wife who was recovering from a cesarean section. As can be expected in the first family death of a young 40 years old professional son with great potential in whom the family had great dreams, many lives were shattered, especially that of my mother who never quite recovered until she died 14 years later. My younger siblings were all in great shock and disbelief. His wife and everyone else were all looking up to me as the eldest child in the family of 10 children, for emotional support and guidance. The other reason is that I was already in the counseling support ministry with my church. As best as I could, and with so many things to be taken care of and funeral arrangements to be made, I stayed calm, composed and on top of everything until a month after the funeral and everyone was processing their grief well. I guess when I noticed that everyone else was settling down and gradually moving on, and with some time and space to myself, it suddenly dawned on me that the brother and friend I used to turn to for emotional support was no longer there. A month from my brother's death I literary crumbled and landed in a hospital with severe back ache, complete emotional drain and a deep sense of loss and grief. I cried continuously and was inconsolable. Gradually, I came to terms with my loss and ganged up with my siblings and parents for comfort and survival through this major transition to a life without our brother. At this stage, shock is protective and enables us to grieve in our own way and comfortable pace.

Denial is a common reaction to almost everyone when we hear of a death. Our intervention in helping the grieving person should include providing a calm and reassuring presence, a quiet and soft atmosphere that allows the information to sink in gradually and pave way for the grieving process in a healthy way. It is hard and even unnecessary to force people out of this stage and the truth is that gradually reality will hit home. If the grieving person is hysterical, let them do it but remain present and visible, giving water, soft drinks, coffee a shoulder to lean on or whatever else they may need for support and comfort at that instance.

2. **Anger**

Depending on who is being mourned, anger may be manifested in many forms and against different people. Even in the case of believers, most often there is anger against God for not protecting their loved ones from maybe an accident, murder, or even for not healing them from a serious illness that might have claimed their life. Questions like "Why me, why now, why my son? Why would God allow such a cruel death" etc. will be prevalent even though no answers are available.

It may be in the case of a spouse whose passing away completely overturns the life of the surviving spouse. The husband who was the head of the family and navigated every aspect of his family's life as the main bread winner, is now suddenly and permanently taken away either in an accident, a sudden illness, a terminal illness, through a murder incident or has even taken his own life. Even though these are different causes of death, the surviving spouse might end up very angry at him now that she has to step into his very large shoes, minus his decision making role, protection and direction for the family. The family was so totally dependent on him, or maybe he controlled everything to the dot and the wife has a great challenge trying to find her way around life on her own, making a living, handling the children and paying their bills. She is suddenly thrown onto the fast moving wheel of life with no warning or preparation and feels overwhelmed or even threatened. She may also be angry at herself for not paying attention on how things were done. She may also get angry at her children who are suddenly looking up to her even for things their father did for them in his lifetime. The children may also be angry at having to live on without the protective father figure. The absence of the role model that he may have been is a scary thought. But more than anything having to readjust their lifestyle because a major life resource is suddenly missing is almost unimaginable.

A wife also dies leaving behind a young husband with young babies or children. Until her death, the wife planned all the household activities including grocery shopping, children's clothing or school needs. She supervised children's homework, attended their school events and took them for all doctor's appointments etc. She cooked, did laundry and planned all family celebrations and vacations since her husband was busy at work making a living for his family. Suddenly she passes away in an accident, at child-birth, or succumbs after a long battle with cancer or whatever else took her life. The husband is in a complete shock, almost in total disbelief that death has actually taken away the pillar of his family existence. He cannot imagine life for himself and their children without her and is beginning to feel cheated at the whole event. He might initially even be angry at God who seems not to care what will happen to his family or how he is expected to play the role of a mother and father all at once without any prior notice or preparation. The husband may even be angry at his deceased wife for leaving everything to him on top of his own previous heavy responsibilities. I can only imagine the kind of thoughts that cross his mind as well as those of their children towards a baby who is herself left behind at birth where the mother dies as a result of birthing complications. Perhaps this baby will experience anger and rejection from all angles as the cause of the mother's death unless the family is helped and supported from such a mind-set. The anger could even be projected against the medical personnel, his parents and other close relatives and friends offering to help. This can easily affect many other relationships and friends that were common to both who may be less and less available to the surviving family due to work and their own family responsibilities. The family ends up not only missing their mother or wife, but also her friends and sometimes relatives who visited mainly because of her. Anger may also result from the fact that they cannot comfortably participate in all the things that she usually initiated without the painful reminder of her absence. However, some people may find peace and comfort and visiting such places as a way of remaining connected to the deceased spouse or parent, doing the things they enjoyed doing together. Great care and support needs to be availed to the surviving family who may be initially be afraid of losing the only living memory of a departed spouse or parent in each other. This may be a very destructive stage of grief where the angry grieving person may be very rude and abrasive in language and reactions to anyone who comes too close to them. It is wisdom to give them some space, but not abandon them completely when they actually need help most. I'm reminded of Job's friends who came to comfort him (Job2:11-13), but seeing how deep his grief was, sat silently for seven days without saying a word. They represent the first chaplains or pastoral caregivers who gave a ministry of their presence until Job was comfortable enough to grieve outwardly in the open.

Intervention at this point may often be tough and complicated to help the grieving person(s). In our efforts to intervene and help, we must be careful not to be experienced as judging and least caring. One of the most supportive ways is to listen attentively and validate the reasons for the anger being projected instead of reacting harshly. While anger is often viewed as a bad reaction, it may at times be a gift and an expression of trust by the grieving person in that they can trust you with their emotions and your willingness to help where you can. In other incidences as in divorce, loss of a job and livelihood or a diagnosis of a terminal illness, anger may actually be projected to the least expected and closest family or friends. The best and most helpful gift to the grieving person(s) at this point may be your patience and silent compassion and not taking it personally. However, when anger becomes destructive, it may be necessary to set up boundaries to protect others who may be attacked unfairly or unexpectedly. "Time Out" may be necessary, explaining that while we are willing to help some changes are necessary for everyone's good before we can continue. If necessary, encourage the hostile grieving person to walk, jog, do some cleaning or watch a movie. Listening to some soothing and calm music might also help. Invite them also to come up with other activities that they know and enjoy that might help them deal with their grief and pain. We as the support system need to remember that acting up on our part will not help to quell the ongoing episodes. We may need to be tough and firm but cannot afford to be swallowed up in the anger.

3. Bargaining

This is the tough stage in which the grieving person bargains with God or whoever they see as their higher power. The terminally ill may be heard praying and pleading with God to give them a second chance with a promise that they would change their lives and live in obedience to God's laws and desires. They might even promise that they will serve in ministry of one kind or the other. It may be that those who are seriously sick as a result of some bad habits like smoking, drug and substance abuse and chemical dependency promise to discontinue all these if God heals them. Some may live to do this successfully while others will do so only for a little while before going back to the same habits that might eventually cost them their lives. The bargaining usually does not hold well for long and is not easily sustainable.

Like Hannah of the Bible, parents have been known to promise God the same that if He heals their sick children they will teach them to love and live for God if they get well. In journeying through abuse and battering in rocky marriages, the abused may also be promising God that if He saves their marriages, they will be better spouses and better role models for others struggling in similar situations. This often brings the abused to a grey area of living in denial and wishful thinking and bargaining. One may even end up hanging on a little too long under hostile brutalities, enduring un-necessary cruelty while hoping for a change of attitude in the abuser. Many times the end result has been death or deep emotional/physical wounds and scars that might otherwise have been avoided. During the bargaining stage, many different characters may be involved. Between couples who have been struggling in their relationships, either may be promising the other that things will improve if the other stopped drinking, recover from serious illness that may be threatening their marriage with death. The same may apply in parent child relationships. I have seen adult children who have for various reasons disconnected from their parents for long periods. Suddenly, they are summoned home because a parent is dying. Some have been heard dealing with guilt and regrets, bargaining and pleading with the dying parents that if they recover things will improve and the son or daughter will stay home to take care of them and sort out whatever had gone wrong between them. The sudden realization that death is really inevitable and there may never be another chance to make up with each other, often results in various family members being frantic and demanding that aggressive measures be taken to sustain a life that may well have already gone in a critical terminal illness, or other tragic life events. These may include fatal accidents, a heart attack or stroke, cancer etc, where nothing can be done to sustain the ending life. Those bargaining may appear to be the most caring or affected, but may actually be dealing with their own guilt, regrets and wishful thinking.

At such times, the only saving grace will be if the patient or dying elderly parent had given specific end of life care instructions to those in the family that walked closely with them through their illness or aging process to avoid unnecessary arguments or divided views. The bargaining person may also be the one dealing with a personal health crisis or is facing consequences with the laws for past misdoings or criminal activities. They may be bargaining with God that if he bails them out of the situation they will shape up and stop their bad habits.

The type of bargaining a person does is often a clue to areas of that person where guilt or unfinished business exists. It may be a quarrel or a misunderstanding that has remained unresolved for many reasons, including lack of inability to forgive from either party. Bargaining could also be someone telling God of all the better things and choices one would do or make if their families were restored or given a chance after a break-up. Even after my separation, I kept praying and hoping that some sudden miracle would bring me and my ex-husband back together, even though he continued harassing me even from a distance. I continued analyzing what I would change and invite him to change and passionately offered these thoughts to God in prayer. An example was for me to be honest and outspoken with my likes and dislikes as things that had continuously hurt me yet for the sake of peace I rarely told him for fear of his anger, but instead I kept piling them up in my heart to a point of unredeemable damage. This went on until he asked for divorce as a final blow to my continued hopes for reconciliation. Like many others in my circumstances, I lived in denial always hoping against hope.

In our intervention, we must realize that in this stage those battling with grief may intentionally keep themselves very busy to avoid or delay facing or dealing with their grief and the pain of their loss as they should. Those helping them must be willing to listen even to the unspoken pain and be attentive to any thing they might do after this to hurt themselves on realizing that it is too late to achieve their bargains. Caringly explain to them that their feelings of guilt and wishful thinking are a normal and genuine part of the grieving process. If on the other hand their grief is justified, help them get to a point of forgiving themselves and others in order to be able to move on. It may be necessary to refer them to their spiritual leaders for further guidance and nurturing.

4. **Depression.**

Depending on what is causing depression in one's life, reality will gradually hit home. It may be expected in the case of a major terminal illness where the patient has gradually declined to a point of total helplessness and poor quality of life for several years or months. Some may even have been in a hospital, a nursing home etc. Changes may have happened in their health clearly indicating that their vital organs were slowly shutting up and they may even be on a ventilator. They may also have started refusing food or medicine and constantly saying that they are "ready to go home". Some may suddenly withdraw and ask to be left alone or even become hostile and unpleasant. They may also appear depressed and praying for God to take them out of their misery. Those with spouses, children or elderly parents dependent on them may be torn apart with moments of wanting to get well and back in circulation with their loved ones while at other moments they feel too sick and wanting out of their situation. They may be anxious and worried about the fate of their loved ones when they die. All these situations often lead to feelings of depression and great anxiety where the grieving person does not know what to ask for from God. They may go through episodes of agitation, deep sadness, sleeplessness, and many episodes of unexplained crying. While all this is going on with the sick or dying one, the family or caregivers may start picking up clues of real decline and imminent death soon. These may quickly trigger up all kinds of depressive reactions from different people and the whole atmosphere may become very volatile and charged with fear, uncertainty and anticipatory grief. The pain of having to let go of the dying loved one and the thought of a future life without them must be painful and depressive. Some caregivers and family members, who have concentrated all their time and focus in the care of this person, might start panicking as to what they will do when death eventually carries their loved one away. There may be a deep sense of emptiness and meaningless life in the anticipation of the sick person's absence. The fear of the unknown future without one's long time spouse, parent or one's child may linger on for months after they are long gone. All these can quickly result in serious depression if care and intervention are not given.

One way of intervening is helping the grieving person to see that their feelings are normal in their journey with grief and that you are willing to walk with them until they feel more comfortable with their situation. Let them know also that they may be in and out of this for unspecified periods until depression gradually fades away. Depression may also be a positive reaction in the healing process as it allows the grieving person to experience their pain and loss realistically and truthfully.

In some cases, depression may be so severe, affecting the grieving person, family and friends and isolating them to the extent that medical intervention may become necessary. Emotional support, empathy and education are all very helpful and significant elements of healing recovery of the grieving person(s).

5. <u>Accepting:</u>

Inevitably, the mourner begins to face the hard reality emotionally and intellectually that their loved one is indeed gone and is no longer physically present in this life. In other cases the grieving person realizes that they are really divorced and each person must now face life alone after many years of married life. Others suddenly face the permanence of their paralysis, amputation or blindness, where they can no longer do all the things they automatically and easily did and took for granted in the past like all of us.

Accepting does not in any way indicate that we like what has happened to us or the losses we have encountered. It just means we have accepted the reality of our loss and grief and will try to find ways and means or redirecting our energy to our future gradually, instead of permanently focusing on the past. It is a step of reconciling ourselves with the reality and finding a way to cope and move on with life as best as may be humanly possible. This is the time the grieving person faces the need to adapt to the new environment. There will be new challenges of being a single parent again, rethinking and reorganizing the parenting styles to adapt to your new life. There may be the initial resentment of these new roles so suddenly imposed on the grieving person by each individual circumstances, while at the same time realizing that the best one can do is reconcile with the situation and move on with life as best as possible.

When the grieving person accepts and reconciles themselves to the new roles and responsibilities, they will feel better and more comfortable with their healing process. There will still be days which are harder than others, but the best one can do is take one step one day at a time. After the worst emotional storm that took all their energies is over, it will be possible to see some light at the end of the tunnel and feel some sense of hope for better days ahead. It will be wise at that point to reinvest their emotional energy into new assignments, hobbies, new friendships and other activities that will begin to shape the new person in a new horizon of life. It will get better and more comfortable to start navigating one's life into new directions, making future plans without the guilt of abandoning the memories of their departed loved one or even their past lives. At this point, the grieving person will be more confident in looking at new and different opportunities in life with a sense and desire of healing oneself and those dependent on them.

Our faith and trust in a God who can strengthen us for each small step or day, carry us through our challenges when we can barely walk. The words of "The Footprints" may be our best help through such crossroads of life. It may literary be a journey of "one little step at a time". It may at times feel like one is taking two steps forward and one step backward resulting in a very slow healing process, until we are strong enough and feeling confident about our process. This season of grief and bereavement varies from person to person based on many reasons and what loss one is grieving. There is not a firm set of rules on how to go through all this but it depends on individuals.

This stage may also facilitate the healing process, developing of a new environment of personal growth, new relationships and activities. It also brings a new hope for better and manageable days ahead. As we learn to accept our losses of one kind or another, we are able to seek new directions in life while remembering our past loses with less pain. Sifting through our memories to see what we can carry from our past to enrich our future and what needs to be discarded for ever to avoid being shackled by the pain of our past for ever. This gradually empowers and encourages us to seek new opportunities to help us continue with our dreams little by little, at times even sustaining the legacies of our loved ones now gone before us. We learn to live with their good memories that might even become support pillars and strengths for us in the future. One can never quite forget the pain of losing, but one gradually begins to accept the fact that perhaps it was good that our loved ones were healed in a different way, never to suffer any more. We can gradually acknowledge these feelings without guilt.

In our intervention, we need to reassure the grieving person that grief is very personal and they must allow themselves to go through it at their own comfortable and manageable pace. Help them understand too that accepting the death of a loved one and getting reconciled with this or other losses in life is not to be viewed as forgetting them or pretending that whatever else we lost in life did not hurt us. Accepting and beginning to look forward into the future, even after a divorce, loss of important limbs like arms and legs, loss of our sight or any major disability is actually a good sign that the journey of healing is finally beginning. Inevitably, there will be many obstacles along the way, but with God on our side and with the help of friends, families and other professionals and support systems availed to us, and we will gradually begin to see some light of hope and healing at the end of our tunnel of grief and loss. However, every grieving person must be patient with themselves and others in this process which is a life changing journey. Like David, (Psalm 121 verses 1, 3 & 8) we will do well to "Look up unto the mountains, does my help come from there?", "He will not let you stumble and fall; the one who watches over you will not sleep". Remembering too that, "The Lord keeps watch over you as you come and go, both now and for ever ". I would want nothing more than the assurance that God will be there for me at all times, even when I am too broken to pray or do anything for myself because "His plans for my life are good, they are good and not for disaster, to give me a future and a hope" Jeremiah 29 verse 11 (KJ Version).

a) Physical Symptoms

There all kinds of physical manifestations of grief and bereavement including too little or too much sleep, loss of appetite, fatigue, unexplained pains and aches everywhere, etc. Unless these issues are adequately and promptly dealt with, there is a likelihood of them resulting in long term problems long after the grieving period. They could very easily change the grieving person's lifestyle from being healthy and active to being withdrawn, dull and sedentary in an unhealthy way.

b) Emotional Symptoms

These symptoms include panic attacks, depression, sadness, numbness, disbelief, hostility, anger, loneliness, emptiness, shock, decreased self-esteem, jealousy, disorientation, helplessness, hopelessness, self-hate, feelings of rejection, withdrawal from others, confusion etc. Grief is wanting and loving those that are dear and precious to our hearts and lives, never wanting to let go of them. After a long illness, there may be relief for self and deceased, often accompanied by a sense of guilt for such feelings. All this is normal and natural part of grieving. There will also be moments of inability to concentrate and focus as we reflect on the absence of the touch and voice of our beloved now gone beyond the grave.

c) Spiritual Symptoms

Regardless of whether the grieving person is a believer or not, the initial shock and impact of grief will often trigger anger against God for allowing the death while we have been praying and trusting Him for healing. At the same time, the spirit will be deeply and passionately seeking God's comfort, consolation, encouragement and help to survive the loss to death. It is wise to allow ourselves and those we may be trying to comfort, console and support to express their feelings in order to clear their minds, empty themselves of the anger and thus be able to look up to God as a helper and not an enemy in the tragedy. Participation of the grieving persons, however young or old, in the funeral arrangements and other rituals will help them to come to terms with the reality of their loss. This will also help them come to some form of closure and move towards some new meaning to life without the deceased loved one.

d) Behavioral Symptoms

During the initial shock of grief and bereavement, some people will deal with it by avoiding and blocking the memories and reality of the situation for a while. Some will cry ceaselessly while others will become motionless and void of emotions. Even these are normal and natural reactions that must not be ridiculed or viewed as stupid. It is important to honor and acknowledge our own or other people's individuality in moments of intense grief and bereavement and allow each person to process their grief in whichever way they feel comfortable. These are the same reasons why we see many behavioral variations of highs and lows of grief during major holidays and anniversaries.

It also helps to remind the grieving person that "*Jesus wept*" (John 11:35) He was grieving the death of his close friend Lazarus. He gave us permission to express our sorrow and pain in tears. Isaiah also refers to Jesus in Isaiah 53:3 as "*A man of sorrows Acquainted with bitterest grief*". We can therefore trust Jesus to understand our heartaches and grief because he has his own first hand experience. God our father_understands too, having experienced a grief too deep and painful that He looked the other way when his son was dying on the cross at Calvary covered with all the sins of humanity.

In general, there is no set timetable for grief. The depth and impact of grief depends on the kind of relationship that existed with the deceased loved one. There is a common saying that "Time heals all the wounds". For some it does but for some it does not and there is no telling how long the pain and intensity of their loss will linger on. All we can do is hang in there until the situation slows down and becomes manageable. It is therefore very important to wait before making any major decisions while the mind is still confused and cannot focus realistically or rationally.

5

ANTICIPATORY GRIEF FOR THE TERMINALLY ILL AND THEIR CAREGIVERS

When a patient receives the diagnosis of a terminal illness like cancer of any kind, major debilitating heart ailments and many others, the shocking news often sends messages of a death sentence; images of a life soon coming to an end however long or short the illness may take before death finally strikes. I cannot even try to imagine the kind of painful thoughts that must run through the minds of the patient at that instance and from then on.

There may be anger at the possibility of not being able to live long enough to achieve one's dreams and aspirations like everyone else in life. I am thinking of a parent who has so many plans for the growing family. Dependent on the age of the children, there must be wonderings and panic attacks as to what will happen to their young children once they die. Terminal illnesses have been known to strike suddenly into the life of an engaged couple with well advanced wedding arrangements with a hope for a bright and long future in marriage together. Suddenly there is need to continue with the arrangements knowing that they may only be together in their marriage for a brief moment before one takes over the compounded role of a caregiver/spouse. Many of the original plans about their future must then be altered in many ways to help cope with the terminal diagnosis.

Anticipatory grief may strike into the life a young and excited person newly graduated, lots of plans and expectations for a bright professional life ahead with the sky as the only limit. The impact of such news must inevitably be devastating after many years of hard work and sacrifices to achieve their academic heights only to realize they might not live long enough to enjoy the fruits of their labors or even make the differences they anticipated albeit in a little way for their families or communities. At the prime of their age, many people at this stage in life have found such news and the anticipatory grief too much to bear and have quickly taken their lives or gone into total depression, helplessness and hopelessness (dependent on their diagnosis, especially the irreversible/incurable HIV/AIDS) resulting in suicides in many cases.

Anticipatory grief for any family or individual can be so debilitating that it almost halts everyone's life, current or future plans both in private or public life. The fear of not knowing what the impact and progression of the illness will be like may be the hardest thing for the patient and the caregiver to contend with. The impact that complicates the grief may vary from finances, how slow or fast the health will decline, what complications may arise, the management of the patient's care and the needs of the other affected family members. It may be that the terminally ill patient is an adult child who has been caring for elderly parents.

These parents must be drastically affected and threatened by such news and begin to grieve a future without their child/caregiver. The child/caregiver must also begin to grieve the pain of perhaps dying earlier and leaving helpless parents behind.

For both the terminally ill and the caregiver, the challenge is to shift and change their past lifestyle to accommodate the new needs for care, be able to focus on and act differently on the emotional, behavioral, psychological and spiritual mindsets that may now appear as this journey continues. The past and current interpersonal relationships between everyone in this circle will be major determining factors as to how they live and relate for the remaining part of their life together. The life and future of everyone involved will change one way or the other. The initial period may be turbulent and feel like they are thrown into a whirlpool of activities and changes, not knowing how things will be like when things finally fall into place. This is when the presence of a higher power like God for believers becomes a paramount necessity to bring some kind of meaning and normalcy to the life ahead and maintain some stability to continue. Support from friends and family will also go a long way under these circumstances. Everyone involved will get to a point of accepting the reality that this diagnosis is not changing and that sooner this terminally ill person will be gone for good. Along the way, changes must be made to care for them and take over some of the responsibilities they handled for themselves and their families. Those remaining behind must now face the reality of life ahead minus the sick spouse, parent, child or even a close/best friend and confidante. This may be the toughest stage in this journey because people walk their grief and part of the morning along the way even before death takes their loved one away. However, some people go through it in denial, hoping against hope that the sick person will heal and life will continue as normal as always. Everyone in this circle may get into some frantic activities trying to make the best use of the remaining time, make it up to each other or even make necessary plans for the future of the ailing patient and the survivors thereafter. The issue of acceptance and facing the reality of this matter determines a great deal what happens in everyone's future. In some cases, prayerfully and with support from everyone involved, both parties are able to walk through this "valley of the shadow of death" (Psalm 23:4) and will in some cases start doing "their good-byes", exchange forgiveness and blessings towards each other and even develop greater yearnings for whatever would pave a way for them to meet and live together in eternity after the separation that death brings. Many hard headed people who ignored salvation and the need for God have been known to suddenly call for and seek God when everything they thought invaluable now appears truly perishable and temporal as we all are. Dealing with anticipatory grief does not mean one will not grieve after the death of the terminally ill patient. Anticipatory grief may even trigger or revive past grief or bereavement that was not adequately dealt with and brought to some kind of closure. Some people grieve in the open while others do it in private and don't even want anyone to ask or talk about it with them. Tradition, culture and age may also dictate how we express our grief and bereavement.

When the terminally patient finally dies, there will still be the initial shock and finality of a journey through the illness. The intensity of the grief will be dependent on many dynamics like the relationships that existed, whether there are any unfinished businesses or grudges and the support around for the survivors and the caregivers whose lives might feel empty and meaningless for a while until they pick up their own lives gradually and continue as best as they can. The intensity of the grief will gradually decrease but should not be measured or compared with anyone else. One gradually finds a time and place to laugh, joke, cry, or just have fun somewhere along the future. These should be viewed as normal and necessary points of the healing process and no one should be condemned for such feelings. They are actually necessary signs and symptoms of acceptance of the situation and that gradual healing is taking place. Do not hurry the process, but be ready to walk this path one step at a time. Days will be different and so will be the moods.

Mr. Stephen Levine cautions us that *"Unattended sorrow narrows the paths of our lives"* It will therefore be a hindrance to our healing and progress in the future. Un-acknowledged grief may eventually be our worst enemy into the future.

We must therefore allow ourselves to feel our grief, be it anticipatory, current or in the future. Only the grieving or bereaved person knows the real implications and depth of their loss and they should be allowed to deal with their bereavement individually. No two people will grieve or mourn in the same manner even in the case of two parents who are both struggling with the loss of their child. Neither will two siblings go through the same emotions at the loss of a common parent. Different genders, age groups, social groupings, cultural backgrounds affect how different people deal with their losses. No one should be made to feel ashamed of their tears or brokenness at moments of grief and loss. At any rate these are necessary responses in the days, months, years and life ahead as the affected persons work towards some form of normalcy in their shattered lives thereafter. Complicated grief may also result from the death of a parent, sibling or ex-spouse with whom we should have had better relationship. Our dreams and hopes of reconciling for a happy ending may surface and disturb us. At the time some people feel like the deceased "haunts you from the grave". We must find a way of completing this grief. In order to move on with life, complete our unmet hopes and dreams and expectations that were not previously achieved. It may take experiencing the unfinished events in order to tell them what you would have said, if you had been given a chance or had known how to do that. "There is sacredness in tears. They are not a mark of weakness but of power. They speak more eloquently than 10,000 tongues. They are the messengers of overwhelming grief, of deep contrition and unspeakable love". (Washington Irving.)

Kept on the inside, tears turn into more bottled heartache and ceaseless pain. Allowed to flow freely, they are cleansing, relieving and healing to the soul. Tears are as old as God's creation and neither could Jesus resist the need to weep when he received the news of the death of his great friend Lazarus from his sisters Martha and Mary. (John 11:35). Jesus therefore knows fully the pain of grief and loss

6

Major Depression and Complicated Grief

This is also known as unresolved grief. After the loss of a loved one, it is common for people to experience a deep sense of sadness, bouts of crying, anger, pain and even depression. Unless one is careful and surrounded by caring and understanding family and friends, about 1 in 5 bereaved people will develop major depression. However, depression can be handled with medicine, counseling or other forms of therapy of one's choice. But it is very important that something is done about it before it is too late and the grieving person becomes suicidal or self-destructive. Some symptoms of complicated grief are:

- continued disbelief in the death of the loved one

- inability to accept the death

- flash-backs, nightmares, memories that keep intruding into thoughts over time

- severe prolonged grief symptoms: anger, sadness or depression

- keeping a fantasy relationship with the deceased with feelings that he/she is always present, watching or haunting

- continuous yearning and searching for the deceased

- unusual symptoms that seem unrelated to the death (physical symptoms, strange or abnormal behavior)

- breaking off ties to social contact and withdrawing from everything

In cases of divorce and separation, your "less loved one" may still be alive. You will need to find ways of healing your past pain, even when your ex-spouse will not change. You must look beyond the loss and be intentional about moving on with life before things get too complicated to handle. You will bring better value and meaning into your own life, removing the shackles and limitations of painful reminders of a relationship that never lived up to your expectations. Regardless of whether one's grief emanates from the death of a loved one or other painful experiences in life like divorce and separation, here are some symptoms of major depression that cannot be explained by normal bereavement:

- constant thoughts of being worthless or hopeless

- ongoing thoughts of death or suicide (other than thoughts that they would be better dead or should have died with their loved one)

- being unable to perform day-to-day activities

- guilt over things done or not done at the time of the loved one's death

- delusions (beliefs that are not true)

- hallucinations (hearing voices or seeing things that are not there) except for "visions" in which the person briefly hears or sees the deceased

- slower body responses and reactions

- extreme weight loss or gain

- symptoms lasting more than 2 months after the loss

Considering that the intense grief and loss alone is enough to negatively impact anyone's health, it is important that anyone experiencing any of the above symptoms consults or seeks help from qualified health or mental health professionals. Proper treatment is imperative because people dealing with complicated or unresolved grief have a much higher risk of an emotional mental breakdown or becoming worse and suicidal. Life might even seem to have come to a standstill for the grieving person and they will need someone to shake them from the daze.

7

DIFFERENT KINDS OF LOSSES

Feelings of loss are very personal and the only person who can fully describe their significance is the one who is personally experiencing or undergoing them. As mentioned earlier, there are many losses and challenges as we travel through life that result in grief, other than just the death of a loved one, be it a family or friend. Again, the extent of the grief each will cause is dependent on the value of what is lost and the implications of its loss and absence from our lives. Such losses will include:

Death of a parent/child	Death of a spouse	Death of a partner
Death of a roommate	Death of a sibling	Death of a close friend
Death of a relative	Death of a colleague	Death of a classmate
Death of a pet	Serious illness of a loved one	Broken Relationships
Loss of innocence in rape etc.	Loss of health through illness	Loss of mental ability
Loss of financial security	Leaving Home	Change of a job
Loss of physical ability	Graduation from school	Loss of a home

Unfortunately, as humanity advances in civilization and technological knowledge, there will be increased new losses to be grieved by each of us. Traditions and cultures of the world continue to change in many ways. Some have proved worth and necessary doing away with. But the loss of some of our traditions and cultures have seriously depleted and minimized our family support systems to the extent that many children and elderly members are lonely and helpless because the aspect of the extended families is less and less. I can only imagine the grief of those who grew up in such surroundings, those who knew the positive impact of extended families, but now have to fend for themselves in their own old age. I will however, highlight just a few of the above mentioned losses and the grief they bring to people's lives today.

GRIEVING THE DEATH OF A CHILD:

When you lose a child you lose your future.

Compassionate Friends say the loss of one's child, our future and hope, is the worst anyone should ever have to endure. It exposes one to deep spiritual battles and questions, deep anger at God and life, including those around us. It brings guilt that our genetic compositions might have endangered our child whether born prematurely, dead or whether they die later. A child's death may also trigger the guilt of not caring for one's child properly and protecting them from all harm in some unfortunate circumstances. One may also feel guilt that our choices and family lifestyles killed our children and the ensuing grief may be unbearable. Others conclude that perhaps God punished our wrong doings by killing our children.

The most painful reality is that even though it happens often, no parents have ever expected to bury their children and then continue living after that. It should be the other way around. Guilt and grief may also result from the fact that the parent old and far gone in life, is still alive instead of a child who dies too early even before their lives "begin". These feelings of grief will still arise, even when a child has been terminally ill right from their birth and they were never expected to live long. There is always a feeling of hoping against hope that this child will somehow outlive the parent. It happens many times over, that after the death of one's child young or as an adult, parents have been known to lose interest in life, start declining and die soon after that. In an Emergency Room incident, when a little 2 year old boy was rushed in with a full arrest only to lose his battle to a heart disease, I heard a heart broken father say in the midst of his painful sobbing *"Something died in me when my son stopped breathing and I don't know if I will ever recover from this loss".* We were informed later that this little toddler had already undergone two heart surgeries and was scheduled to go through a third one in two weeks time. But even though all along the parents and the large family that came had known he was critically ill, it was still an unbearable loss that crashed all those of us present in the ER that fateful morning. Many have been heard to say that life has lost its meaning after such a loss. I know this for a fact, having watched my own mother completely lose herself when my brother (2nd born in a family of 10 children) died instantly in a motor vehicle accident. Even though my mother lived for another 12 years after that, she was never the same and would speak about him constantly. Grief took a great toll on her and my father after the death of yet another of my younger brother as a result of a liver problem. My father quickly went down with his grief and my mother who was his immediate caregiver with our back-up succumbed to grief four months after my father's death. Both of them were very open and frank with me that their children's deaths were the worst that could happen to them. My mother openly told me one day in a conversation that she did not want to live long enough to have to burry any one else after that. Within three weeks of saying this to me, my mother passed away.

Sudden or unexpected death comes with great denial and disbelief as in a motor vehicle accident. There is trauma and shattered dreams for the diseased child. If a child dies in a homicide or accident, there will be various complications in the grieving process for the family and friends. The involvement of a coroner and other legal implications, going to the courts, listening to and giving testimonies, further prolongs and complicates the grieving process for the family and everyone else involved in the loss.

The grieving parent may be left deeply angry that the person who killed their child is still alive and might still have a second chance to life after serving their prison sentence while their child's life is brutally terminated for ever. This may also result in anger against God for not protecting their child from this sudden death. In some very sad situations, especially where family relations were already tense and not agreeable, such a sudden death could turn into a vicious cycle with different family members blaming each other for not being there. Many marriages have been known to break down with this as the last straw.

It is not unusual to find a grieving parent commit suicide or do some drastic things either to self or others as they struggle with the anger and guilt of being alive while their child who deserved to live is dead. Mothers have been known to reject other surviving children, even refusing to nurse babies in their torment of loss and grief. It is at this time that pastoral care givers and everyone around such grief need to be extremely careful not to rationalize the situation. At times it is best just be a silent support and presence until the intensity of their grief subsides and they can start dealing with it better. In our anxiety to say something, we may end up doing greater damage than help. Great patience and compassion will be needed.

Long term illness in children has a very deep effect as they journey through some very turbulent and intense places of pain, confusion and helplessness. It is equally devastating for any parent or guardian to watch them helplessly suffer in and out of the hospital yet knowing there is nothing you can do to change the situation other than encourage, remain present and make them as comfortable as possible. This is even harder in the case of a child who is born with a life threatening condition that will be their journeying companions till death. During this period, if there are other children in the family, they may feel left out as all the attention is on the sick one until they finally pass away.

When this child finally dies, the family might be torn between feeling a sense of relief that this child is at rest and not suffering any more. But guilty feelings may also creep into their lives wondering if there is anything they might have done differently in their care. But gradually, as the situation gets better, the parents and others in the family might benefit from getting involved into a support group of other parents who have gone through such an experience or loss. But we do need to constantly remember that grief is very personal and how we grieve will very much depend on the personal relationships we had with our departed loved one.

Grieving the Loss of a Spouse:

When you lose your spouse, you lose your present.

The death of a spouse is an earth shattering blow that brings incomprehensible pain. This often means the loss of your best friend and the most intimate relationship, bridge partner, companion and your hope for the future. This means the end of that passionate goodnight kiss, the straightening of a tie as you leave home for work or for a meeting or a reassuring pat on the shoulder. When a life partner dies, your identity dies with them. You are soon given a new identity as a "widow or a widower". These become labels that communicate a very harsh reality, and some unbearable sadness. Yet in many cases the people around widows and widowers are not even aware of this fact.

Discovering who you are after a death of a spouse

The loss of a spouse to death quickly moves the surviving spouse from the category of "married" to "widowed. As in all other loses, it is a transition in life without preparation and often times with no fore-warning. It challenges the widowed to restructure their lives following this enormous change. It sets you on a path to redefine yourself and create a whole new landscape or new uncharted territory for your future. It is a defining moment for who you will become. Newly widowed, one is called to blaze a new trail for their lives from this point forth. You will need to renegotiate everything as one who will be living on your own, with decreased options.

The death of a spouse tears through every layer of one's existence.

Losing a spouse is most often losing one's best friend. Some of the physical manifestations of the impact of your grief may include – ulcers, colitis, rheumatoid arthritis, rapid heartbeat, high blood pressure, back pain, dizziness, etc. Your immune system may also be compromised resulting in intermittent colds and other minor illnesses. Anger at God, at the loved one who died, your family and everything else may also be part of your grieving process. This too is normal. Be honest with God about it as you pray for help because He knows and understands exactly what you are going through, even when those around you want to but cannot fully appreciate the depth of your loss. (Psalm 22:1-2, 19)

The scars from your grief and the healing process from your loss will ALWAYS be a part of your life from this time forth. It will be part of your new identity. However grief does not have to be the defining factor for the quality of the rest of your life. It is okay to live, learn and gradually to love again as time goes by. You can incorporate your loss and use it to forge a new identity that helps you continue growing. Your faith traditions can also help giving meaning to loss, and the hope of an eternal connection to your loved one. As you choose to ritually mark your grief during important anniversaries and holidays, it will allow for a softening of the repeated reminders of your loss.

Learn new skills, meet new people, take up new hobbies and intentionally strive to live on as best as God helps you. Perhaps this is what your departed spouse would actually want you to do. To continue the dreams and projects you started and enjoyed together.

It will be necessary to learn to live with and accommodate your loss and make it a part of who you are. It is a part of your new identity that needs to be embraced and accepted. It may be tough at the beginning but necessary for your healing. Good self care will include eating balanced and nutritious meals; enough rest, regular exercise, taking some necessary vitamins, etc. Get your regular medical checkups, especially if you had been putting them off as you focused all your time, resources and energy on the care for your loved one.

You are not alone in your widowhood. However, acknowledge the uniqueness of your personal situation. The uniqueness of your sorrow may come from

> Length of your marriage
> The age of your spouse
> Circumstances of death
> Your gender and age
> Your family's coping mechanism & communication style
> Cultural & religious orientation
> Financial, social issues
> Children or no children

Embrace your situation. Honor it. Affirm its reality. While grief is devastating, it is also fertile ground for some mystical experiences. Only then will you be able to pick up the broken pieces of your life and move on.

Acknowledge the many losses caused by the death of your spouse in order to refocus and make NEW BEGINNINGS.

Not only is this a physical loss of your spouse, but also:

The loss of your high school sweet heart
Your first love
Your best friend and confidante
Your lover & soul-mate
Your dance partner & traveling companion
Your chef, your gardener, your chauffeur, your accountant
Your comedian, encourager, pillar of strength,
And many other roles they played in your life.

Being single again, no matter how long or short you have been married is DIFFERENT. But you do not become any less important, nor should you allow others to make you feel that way for any reason. Loneliness is something nobody wants to experience, but it will be inevitable at the beginning. But the Lord promises to stay with you and help you through your grief. He will not abandon you. (Psalm 139:1-17), (John 14:18-19). He will watch your going out and your coming back, both now and for ever. (Psalm 121:8)

Rediscovering Purpose & Meaning in Life:

The measure of your grief is the measure of how much you loved your dearly departed spouse. While their absence hurts as deeply as you loved them, I'd rather that was my experience rather than the painful regrets from unfulfilled life and dreams.

Our grieving is part of life, not something removed from it. It is gradually transformed into something closer to remembering and cherishing with gratitude, a warm comforting glow instead of a hot burning fire. As you go deeper into your pain, you encounter persons, events, words, elements of creation that bring small nuggets and graces of healing. Trust this sacred rhythm; open yourself to these occasions of grace. They are gracious gifts, gracious assistance for your journey through grief. As you go through these "soul breaking" moments, your deep contemplation of the beautiful relations you had with your beloved, will be the most creative human response to the "shredding of your soul by the grief you feel. Soothe your aching heart with the richness of your memories.

You might want to set a small memorial space in a private corner of your house with a picture of your loved one and some tokens that recall and signify your special relationship. You have not lost the memories that you spun together, nor the impact that your beloved had on your life, the values you learnt from them and the interests you both developed and shared over the years. Watching family videos and family pictures from the past become important and helpful ways to bring back into remembrance some good old days. Some of the memories may be painful reminders at the beginning, but they will one day be precious treasures you will be glad to have. Creating a family heirloom from the relationship you had with your dearly departed will not only be good for your current family members and friends who share your loss today, but also for future generations.

To give healthy and helpful meaning to your new life and New Beginnings, it will help to intentionally give meaning to the life and death of your loved one. The journey will at times take you through some very bumpy places and phases. These may include moments of intense anger, deep sorrow, terrifying fear, etc. The path to the new horizons of your new different life may cause you to feel like a passenger on a long and at times uncomfortable journey that you did not sign up for, but were booked on nonetheless.

In search of meaning and purpose to life, embrace the importance of your faith and spirituality. In an effort to survive and find the necessary support, it may be time to join a regular church family if you do not have one already.

New beginnings encourage you to re-discover a reason to get your feet out of bed, even when you really don't feel like doing so. It propels you to gradually step out of your sorrow, even out of your home, after your life line, your spouse has been terminally and permanently severed. You are encouraged to step out into the track of life and living, praying and trusting God for grace enough for every new day. Just as He promised Joshua of olden days, He will never forsake or leave you alone. Not now, not ever. He will keep you in perfect peace if you can trust him with your future and fix your thoughts on him even for what you think is impossible. (Isaiah 26: 3)

Re-evaluating and Refocusing on Life:

Be aware that the death of a spouse may trigger thoughts of your own eventual death, either because this is a reality for each of us, or because perhaps you too are sick etc.

Give your grief the necessary space and time which differs from person to person. If you stay too busy to grieve, eventually the body will find a way of grounding you from running away. Find a way of balancing between going overboard with too many activities to total resignation and giving up on life for good. Your spirit too is grieving and you might be going through a "dark night of the soul". Remember that a loving God will stand with you in your loss and grief. Those who care about you cannot grieve for you, but they can and are willing to light up the candles to help you find your way through the dark night if you reach out to them. Help them to help you by being honest with them. Don't always say "I'm fine". Let some people know how terribly you actually feel at times. Your grief is real and you should not sugar coat, down play or hide it.

You may not ever get over your grief, but with God's help and the support of family friends and support group, you gradually go through it. The truth is that there is no way over, under or around grief. As you allow yourself to experience grief without "fight or flight' you will notice a gradual change for better. You may be alone on this

ride but never completely as a helpless victim, regardless of how your loved one might have died.

Take heart. While the wound of grief is so painful and we naturally wish it would pass faster than it does, it is a season in which we learn lessons that would not have been possible if we had short-circuited the grieving process. We experience and learn of the incredible resilience of the human spirit. We also find out that if we give grief its dues, sorrow returns the favor by giving us a precious gift – the assurance that we have indeed loved deeply in this lifetime. This is by far the greatest achievement in life. Allow yourself to feel good when those moments come. Happiness is never a betrayal of your love for your departed spouse.

As often as you can, remind yourself of your reasons for living on. You have a future worth enduring for, and you have the right and the reason to feel a renewed sense of purpose and pleasure in your life. Hope in the Lord who will give you a New Beginning, a New Joy and a New Song for your new life ahead. He promises to do you good and restore you for His own glory. (Psalm 40: 1-5)

While you may feel diminished by the death of the one you love, remember that out of that pain, God is birthing an experience of immeasurable value. (Psalm 118: 16-17). You now have the powerful truth of what it is to feel the pain of loosing a loved one.

Like Paul said in 2 Corinthians 1:3-5, as the Lord comforts you through your own sorrow, you will be better equipped to comfort and minister to those who go through this painful passage of devastating loss and grief after you. You also hold the precious knowledge of how important love can be and how vital it is as a source of joy in life – yet how easy it is to take love for granted and overlook the abundance of the love that surrounds you. Sharing that truth can greatly enlarge the lives of everyone around you.

How you actively fill your time through grief will determine whether and how your healing will occur. You will need active attention and mending. Some of the threads that will heal and mend the wound of sorrow will include forgiveness, love, creativity, sharing, relationships with others around you, etc. A healthy and positive attitude will go along way in grief recovery.

Acknowledge your feelings and grief whenever they catch up with you. Spend time with those who allow you to do so without question or judgment. Thoughtfully choose who to spend time with. Give yourself space to weep as necessary, even in private. Jesus wept when Lazarus died. (John 11:35) Your tears are a valuable reflection of the importance of the relationship that is now for ever changed.

While there is need to postpone major decisions, some things must be acted upon regularly. Enlist the help of a family member or a close trusted friend to assist you. Get clear information on insurance, paying bills, savings, debts, inheritance etc.

As time passes, take one step at a time, one day at a time prayerfully. Depending on every individual, things will become better as you learn to accept, receive support from those around you as you process your grief and start New Beginnings. Be grateful for everything you have received and experienced in your life. Be grateful for all the possibilities the future holds for you with God's grace and guidance. Begin to thank God too, for the wonderful memories you will always have of your beloved. Gratitude is an important feeling to weave into your daily life.

As you journey on, pray that every day will become an opportunity for a New Beginning to all that you will now become. Do not allow yourself to be consumed with the guilt of surviving while your loved one died. This is out of your control because God is the giver of life and has everyone's destiny and length of life.

Let the power of prayer become your best and closest companion. No matter how abandoned you will feel at times, God is present with you to the end of your life and compassionately sharing your agony.

As we learn from the words of the poem "FOOTPRINTS", when the pain and sorrow is so deep you can barely take a step, remember He promises to carry you through the deep waters or the hot fires of your sorrow and grief to a safe harbor of healing. He wants to share your burden of sorrow, walk and talk with you along the pathway of healing just like He did with His disciples on the Road to Emmaus. Just as it happened with the disciples, you may be too heart broken to notice or experience His comforting and encouraging presence at that time, but as your sorrow gradually lightens, you will realize He has truly been there for you in many places and forms.

Anchor your spirit to a solid foundation that is one with the force flowing all over the universe to touch hurting souls like yours, rest in the grace of the eternal God. Realize that your grieving is in fact, an encounter with the Eternal, that your broken heart is now an entranceway for God to abide with you. He promises you a rebirth. As your identity changes among your family and friends, your life, with God's help, can take on a new dimension, depth and texture. You can be for ever changed.

I close with the words of Paul in 2 Corinthians 4 verses 7-12.

> *But this precious treasure – this light and power that now shine within us – is held in perishable containers, that is, in our weak bodies. So everyone can see that our glorious power is from God and is not our own. We are pressed on every side by troubles, but we are not crushed and broken. We are perplexed, but God never abandons us. We are hunted down, but God never abandons us. We get knocked down, but we get up again and keep going.*

> *Through suffering, these bodies of ours constantly share in the death of Jesus so that the life of Jesus may also be seen in our bodies.*

Psalm 118:16-17:
> *The strong right arm of the Lord is raised in triumph. The strong right arm of the Lord has done glorious things. I will not die, but I will live to tell what the Lord has done.*

This slight momentary affliction is preparing us for an eternal weight of glory beyond our imagination. As believers, we can live and lean on the hope of spending eternity with God and our dearly departed in a heaven where there will be no more ***death or sorrow or crying or pain.*** (Revelations 21:4) We will never worry about losing them to death again. The challenge now is for us to keep looking up to Jesus and to that heavenly city of God as we too continue our journey. The reality is that we too have a date with death and it matters greatly how we are living every day. The best gift we can give to those surviving us is the sure knowledge of where we are headed after we go beyond the grave. It creates hope after death and something to hang on to.

The sudden or even expected death (from prolonged terminal illness) and the absence of a spouse of many years might leave one feeling as if they are in a non-ending whirlpool of life. No matter how large or small our outside is, we often come to see our partner as the primary source and resource – the one we turn to for acknowledgement, affirmation and comfort, etc. Death in these relationships overturns one's life. Dinnertime or evening

times might have become the sundowner that is suddenly discontinued without any prior notice. Career and social ups and downs was a staple of nightly briefing moments or during the pillow-talk. All manner of loss or gain were generally shared. The person you turned to every time your heart hurt is no longer there for you. Your spouse's death is now the source of the deepest pain you have ever experienced. You are now wondering and fearful of who and where to turn to. Who can even understand what you are really going through?

The death of one's long-term spouse leaves one feeling as if they have literary lost a piece of their own body. Similar heartache and pain might also be provoked by divorce or separation after many years of marriage. The emotions attached to a death or divorce is not defined by time but by the feelings they produced within time. The grieving spouse is suddenly wrapped up in grief and the frightening thought of raising children alone or growing old alone.

It is a common observation that women handle their grief better and remain unmarried for longer or for the rest of their lives. Men often bottle up their grief and behave heroic. On the other hand, older widowers and widows might be ridiculed for dating or remarrying. People tend to forget that even in their senior years, they too need intimacy. Their children also at times go into shock and disbelief forgetting that their widowed parent has needs (emotional, spiritual, sexual etc). However, it is important for the surviving parent to be considerate of the children bearing in mind that they too have lost their father.

Find an appropriate way of sharing your intentions and give them a chance to meet this person you intend to make part of their lives. Allow them some time alone to experience each other. Whether young or old, help your children and family understand that your remarrying does not imply that you did not love their father or mother. On the other hand, if this new person cannot cope with your children, it would be advisable to reevaluate the situation. It is worth remembering that your children will be a part of your life for as long as you live.

At the same time, society is more permissive and understanding towards men than women and will be less criticized if they remarry. Befriending a common friend between the deceased spouse and the grieving spouse will often result in scandals, with suspicion that this relationship might have existed even before the death. In all fairness, no widow or widower should be punished for remarrying and moving on with their lives. It is their life. No one should have the right to make them feel guilty for new found love. There is no "proper" length of grieving time before remarrying either after the death of a spouse or a divorce. The priority and the determining factor should be one's own happiness, not necessarily pleasing others. If there are children, it is wise to reason with them as best as humanly possible, but you have the final word.

Nobody should be compelled to mourn or pay a tribute to a lost life for ever. Some people may enter into a new relationship immediately to help cope with their grief and avoid loneliness and isolation. Too soon may cause its own complications as the mind of the grieving person may still be intensely wrapped around their grief, hampering their capacity to make good decisions or relate comfortably with others. At such times when the grieving person is still very vulnerable, they might easily expose themselves to ill intentioned predators who might take advantage of them.

Build a new "normal" life for yourself.

You know yourself and your coping strengths better than anyone else. As hard as this may be, remember that even though your life companion has passed away, your future was not wiped away. You still have a future, just that it has been somewhat altered from your original path and hopes laid down by you and your late spouse.

Face your emotions.

Grief brings real and not imaginary fears that you cannot simply ignore or wish away. Cry whenever you need to. This is your personal journey of tears and nobody can or should dictate to you on how to process your stress.

Find new friends

As a widow or widower, you might feel uncomfortable and unable to fit into the social circles you enjoyed when your spouse lived. This may be true in some cases, but some of your former comrades might still want to keep up with you and to be in your support system. However, look for widowed people's support group who will understand you and your emotions better. Such support groups may be found in churches, hospitals, hospices and counseling organizations.

Be Safe

As you interact with other people, you will be reassured, encouraged and strengthened. As you depend on God and faith, you will feel stronger and gradually in control of your life again which also helps. Rely on your spirituality as much as possible and let God's love and grace heal, nurture and restore you.

Discover yourself:

However long or short you have lived with your spouse, his absence from your life may leave you feeling very vulnerable in many ways. Insecurity and fear creep in. Allow yourself to take up new responsibilities previously handled by your late spouse gradually. This may include lawn care, plumbing, simple repairs, planning your finances or family holidays. If you feel overwhelmed, feel free to ask for help when necessary instead of suddenly overloading your grieving mind. You will be surprised at how many people are eager to help you but are afraid to offer lest they appear as if they are imposing themselves on you. With time, you will feel better, more confident and happier. Do not allow yourself to feel guilty of all the improvements you are making, but keep the good memories of your spouse and imagine how proud he/she would be to see you doing better.

Imagine the worst

Instead of fretting and panicking about what *may* happen, think what worse could be. You would still survive. It may take changing your lifestyle to cut down on expenses. It may even necessitate selling some things you no longer need in order to keep up with your bills and other financial responsibilities. That may be okay too. Remember the Serenity Prayer. Ask God to help you change what you can and to accept what you cannot change. Do what you have to do and constantly seek God's help and guidance in every step and need.

Encourage yourself in God:

He promises never to leave or forsake you. He also promises in Isaiah 43:19 that he will make a way in the sea. He will also do a new thing in your life.

You never forget. You will carry your beloved with you for ever as a cherished part of who you are, and grow to be more compassionate, appreciative and more tolerant with other people. As you keep facing your fears, you will learn to embrace life again, connecting, laughing and loving again with a full heart.

Grieving the Loss of a Parent:

When you lose a parent, you lose your past.

The loss of a parent, regardless of how old or young one is, must be one of the most disorienting losses. Whether one has been brought up by both parent or by a single parent, the intensity of losing a parent can be devastating. This is the first person(s) that a baby ever gets into contact with before and after birth. These are the first voices, faces and touch that the baby experiences and bonds with that represent security, safety, unconditional love and protection. And even as we mature and grow older, our parents remain a pillar of strength and support in the midst of the storms of life. These are the first people we turn to for affirmation and appreciation. One's parent(s) tend to become a constant point of contact even for those who travel around the world, even into the battlefields all over the world. It is one's parent who will be there to celebrate us when we succeed and support us when we are in trouble. It is not unusual to find that the only people, who are present in a murder or other serious criminal trials, when everyone else has given up, are one's parents. The parent will continue standing by their child even after they are judged and committed to life imprisonment or even to a death-row for their crimes. It is our parents who love us when everyone else give up and want nothing to do with us.

The reality therefore is that when a parent dies, one feels lost and wondering what next, especially for young children still dependent on their parents. Even for adults, it is still hard because we still seek advice and approval from them. There is a deep sense of loss and emptiness knowing that while one can remarry after the loss of a spouse, or have other children after the loss of a child, we have only one biological father and mother in a lifetime. This is not in any way to suggest that you can easily replace either a spouse or a child, but that one can have more than one.

I thought it was tragic enough to lose my two younger brothers, especially as I agonized on what it did to my parents who were still alive. But the death of both parents within 4 months is still the worst grief that I have ever experienced. Odd as it sounds coming from a mature grandmother, I suddenly realized what it feels to be an orphan. I had already gone through a divorce and my parents stood for and with me through the worst situations of my life. They were my heroes in many ways. As I struggled with many life issues, it was the assurance from my father and my mother that they believed in me and were praying for me, that propelled me forward to surviving different crises. I was able to bounce back into life after crashing blows of life as long as my mother was around. I had learnt to trust her with every bit of my life and could confidently bear my struggles and failures without fearing rejection. But for now, I am continuously leaning on the sweet comforting memories of my mother and the nurturing empowering words she told me over the years. As I reminisce on her memories, her strength, values, principles and most of all her faith, telling her stories, I feel comforted as if she is close-by.

As we grieve and miss our parents, it will help to remember some funny moments shared as we were growing up, some heroic deeds in a challenging situation and thank God for them. Perhaps you remember a father sharing something that influenced you and changed your general outlook to life in a moment of great challenge like the loss of a job, a broken relationship or even starting your own family. If he motivated you to move on, thank God for that and use that memory and draw strength from that to move on. It may even be a challenge he gave you to do something you never imagined you could ever do. Your parents might have been the recharging elements whenever you felt like your energies were fading off and you wanted to quit. Let such memories propel you upwards, however slowly it feels. Try to imagine them still cheering you as they did during whatever games you enjoyed with them. Imagine them standing by your bedside praying as you awaited some surgical procedures. I felt some deep sense of peace a little while after my mother died and I had to undergo a major back surgery. At one point I wished she was there like she always did at such moments in her lifetime, praying for me before surgery. I found comfort in remembering and believing that she would always be with me in the spirit ***wherever and whenever*** I yearned for her.

In a case where a parent(s) were either sick or well advanced in age, we may be called to love them deeply enough to want what is good for them even though it may not be good for us. I am thinking of the many times I have been called to support families whose parent is fast declining and every indication shows they will not recover. Sometimes dealing with that reality and with doctors suggesting they need to let the doctors stop the life support so that the parent can rest in peace from what is ailing them. I have found this to be the hardest decision anyone is ever asked to make for a loved one, not just a parent but everyone. This is worse still if the dying person has no living will stating clearly what they would want done for them in such a moment. This is a moment when one is called to overlook your interest of having your parent with you for as long as possible and let them rest out of their sick body and go back to their heavenly home

Unfortunately, their being very old does not exempt us from the pain of losing them to death. There will never be a time when we are completely ready for their absence from our lives. But it calls on those surviving them to be considering what is good for the dying parent and allow God to do His will and take them to their final resting place if the time comes. Life then challenges you, as with all other deaths and loses to adapt to a new life and journey without your parents. The Lord who knows our end from the very beginning will continue to guide and direct our lives long after our parents have gone out of our lives. This may sound impossible when a baby or a young child is left without one or both parents at a very tender age, but one way or the other, God will in His own way ensure that their destiny will be lived as He originally planned for them. Our lives will have to move on, even though drastically altered by the absence of our parents.

When we know and fully understand our own emotional journey, its challenges and the recovering process we will handle our transition in a better and more confident manner. However, when we lose our parents under some tragic unexpected circumstances, accidents, our healing process is definitely altered, complicated and harder to bear. The death of any parent with whom we had good relationships, crashes and breaks our hearts in a way we cannot imagine surviving. It removes all the safety and security we have ever known. To a certain extent, especially in young children, death steals trust, confidence and freedom. This brings back to memory sadness and sorrow for things and people who had died long ago, like grandparents and other close relatives.

As you watch you parents mourn their own parents, you realize that their sorrow was separated only by the tissue of time from what would some day be your sorrow for the loss of your own parents. Part of the grief you feel for your grandparents will be your own anticipatory grief as you wonder how you would survive the death of your own parents whenever it happens. Sometimes it sensitizes people to be careful how they treat their own parents. Suddenly people realize that their parents are also advanced in age and could be gone sooner than later. This is more evident when you lose a grownup sibling and observe the way it completely crashes your parents as they mourn their child who should have survived them. Like in the case of my parents, the death of my second younger brother seemed to be the last straw as we heard our parents say they would not want to live through such an experience again. It seemed to take their motivation to live and they slowly declined in health and both died two years after that.

It may be that you also hear of the death of their age-mates or attend funerals. This puts you through a mental prelude of imagining your parents in similar coffins, images of them dead and even the awful big grave. You begin to have some very vivid imaginations of what might happen to them and what that would mean for you. But when death finally strikes home, all these imaginations are poor and insignificant in the face of the final sufferings and agony of your deep grief and loss.

As your parent(s) takes their last breath, the final layer of your childhood is discontinued for ever. As hard as it is to see them go and perhaps you being called to speak at their funeral, certain thoughts and memories will challenge your silent grief. There will be some things known only to you about them that need to be said in their honor which will land squarely on you to honor them as they are laid to their final resting place. This may be the hardest thing you will ever have to do, but many have said finally they were glad they did that and it gave them an inner peace that also helped come to terms with their parent's death. I can attest to that feeling, having preached at my own mother's memorial service. It was a very emotional thing but I had to honor her request. It is a rare and last chance to stand and redeem your parent's heroic ordinary life. Some feel it is a one last chance to show our parents, family and friends that we can be counted on to stand up for them and carry on their legacy.

Despite of all that is going on, suddenly we discover and realize that we have actually grown up and endured one of the worst heartaches – the death of a parent like many others before you. Other people experience the transformation of life that comes with the grief and loss of a parent. Prayerfully, you must take over the baton from them and continue the race of life from generation to generation. This reminds us of our mortality and the fact that we are now the link between the receding generations to newly developing generations after us.

Apparently, looking at what has happened around our parent's death, one feels the urge to put your own life/house in order. This is especially important if you have a spouse and children. You analyze any and all decisions that might have been left hanging like the Living Will, you main will, etc. If you were personally challenged by these upon your parent's death on top of your deep grief, you will want to ensure that your own family would not have to deal with that upon your own death. This is often referred to as ensuring that you lay clear stepping stones for those who come after you. Do things that would make it easier for your own family and friends in their grieving process. As much as we desire to do a celebration of the life of those that have gone before us, complications from unfinished businesses might make this very hard.

As in any other loses, find ways of remembering your parents and keeping their memories alive for future generations. Depending on the ability of the surviving families, there are many ways of honoring the departed. You can donate to charity in their honor, establishing a foundation or project in memory of them, etc. Find a way of sharing their stories and their achievements. Continue to sustain any projects they started in their lifetime and strive to complete any that they were still working on. Acknowledge the sadness, the fear, the uncertainty you might be experiencing because of this grief and loss. If it is prolonged, seek professional counseling to help you through this phase. Find a grief support group and if necessary one that specifically deals with the loss of a parent. You will find people who can identify with you, empathize with you and walk through the path of grief with you. Gradually, however long or short, the grief may become bearable and you will start reliving the good memories of things you enjoyed doing together with your parent.

While I still miss my father, I am at a point where I thank God for him and remember the many times as I went through my own struggles, and my father's constant affirmation reminding me that he had great confidence in my surviving whatever I was undergoing and coming out victorious because he and my mother were praying for me. I can almost hear his firm voice reminding me that "Penny, you know quitting is not an option for you". Because of his faith in me and wanting so much to honor that, I found myself overcoming challenges I had thought would finish me.

I remember my mother forcing me to sing the "Amazing Grace" with her in the midst of major storms in our lives, and reminding me that God's grace was as fresh and real for me as it was for Paul. One way of experiencing my mother's spirit constantly traveling with me through the jungles of this life is continuing to sing to my patients and families as part of my chaplain's ministry at the hospital or with the hospice. The comfort this brings to them reminds me of my mother telling me that if I focus on the comfort of those hurting, dying and grieving, God will take care of my own grief, pain and struggles in life. This became so real for me after a major back surgery that tremendously slowed me down and really challenged me as I walked around the hospital ministering to patients, families and staff. The more I yearned to be used of God to comfort and encourage those that were grieving, the less I thought about my own pain.

Grieving the Loss of a Sibling:

When you lose a sibling you lose you oldest playmate.

Every loss we experience in our lives leaves a gaping hole. However, the death of a sibling creates an especially tender void. Our siblings are the closest part of our childhood history. Our siblings might even know some very important secrets about us that nobody else knows, not even our parents. They are our very first and closest playmates. A sibling may be the only person we fight with but when someone else tries to get in between, both siblings forget their own disagreements and gang up to fight the "intruder" in defending their sibling. The death of a sibling therefore casts an unusual shadow on our future and their absence from our lives is devastating in its own way.

Our siblings form the very first peer group and so their death remind us of our own mortality, especially when you lose a younger sibling. Siblings play a very important role in our family of origin even after we are grown up. Together, the siblings share the responsibilities of caring for other siblings, younger or older, especially for those that are disadvantaged or challenged by one thing or the other. They share the care of elderly parents. In every family, each sibling has their own unique role in all that happens among them. So when one dies, there is a very definite disruption of life among the surviving siblings and the parents if still alive. If the dead sibling had his/her own family, under normal circumstances, the surviving siblings are expected to take the added responsibilities to watch over his/her family to a certain extent, especially if there are young children. They leave a gap in the caring of their parents if they are still alive which must now be shared between the surviving siblings.

In every family, there are games, jokes, hobbies, and holiday activities unique to the siblings. So the absence of any of them will inevitably affect the rest. As we grieve the loss of our siblings, especially the younger ones, when our parents are still alive, there may be some form of guilt and wishing that you should be the one who died. The devastation and crushing pain of losing a child is the worst to be endured by any parent.

This is the worst blow to watch your own parents battling such grief and you really don't know how to comfort them. At times you are even ashamed to grieve your loss, even though it is real and necessary, around your parents knowing what they are going through. You end up suppressing it and getting so engrossed with other people's grief to the point of neglecting the need to heal your own grief too. Be sure to acknowledge and process it like everyone else. Give yourself time and space to do this. Take time and do whatever comforts you best to remember your sibling. Find the time and place to talk about him/her with your family or friends. Eulogize your sibling if you feel strong enough to do so. Write a farewell letter and tell him anything you wish you had told them before they passed away.

In some instances, sibling rivalry may have left some bitter feelings that were not quite solved before one of them dies. Despite any disagreements, love and affection may still co-exist with rivalry and jealousy. The surviving sibling may experience guilt for the unresolved issues or their inability to care for or protect the one who died. These may be normal feelings which could also be coupled with wishful thinking. The reality is that there is nothing one can do to reverse the clock of life. The best the grieving person can do is to use this as a motivation for positive change in how they treat those still alive around them. One needs to go a step further, forgive oneself and move on as best as humanly possible. Find a way of doing something in memory of your deceased sibling. Support the family they left behind and this will help put some meaning into the relationship that is now gone for ever.

I lost 2 younger brothers, both at their prime age of 40, which left a deep pain in me for many years. I often asked God why He would take them, both leaving very young children, instead of taking me whose children were older. Through my grief, God reminded me of all the concern both my brothers had for me, always challenging me to take good care of me, their elder sister. They had both constantly expressed deep faith in me, one to the extent of telling me that he knew his family would be taken good care of as long as I was there. This was actually long before he died in an accident.

As a result of this, I took it upon myself to do everything I could to care of me and with my other siblings also help educate the nephews and nieces they left behind. This did not mean me forgetting them but doing something to honor them. The surviving sibling(s) might also devise a plan or project in honor of their departed sibling and keep their memory alive. Some options would include making a family scrap book with pictures and stories of the deceased sibling. Highlight their adult life, achievements and the family of their own if any. A foundation in their honor can also be established or money donated to charity that might have interested them during their lifetime. Another way of sustaining their legacy if they left a family behind is working with the surviving spouse and their children to decide what they would want to do in this respect. They might want to do an annual event around the death anniversary in their memory. You can join in such a venture and help to achieve that wish. As you all do this and encourage the support of other family members, you will all be able to process your grief and healing in a meaningful way for all.

The most important thing that the death of a sibling reminds us is our own mortality again. Whether the deceased sibling is younger or older than us, they are still in your generation and that means death can catch up you at any time just as it did with them. As the journey of grief continues, one must get to a point in their loss of whatever kind, when they must choose life and the need to reconstruct their lives beyond their loss. While life without your loved one will never be the same again for you, you can control the way you change – for better or for worse. One will need to choose what is good and necessary to carry over from the past into the future.

Inevitably, something will have to be done away with in order to reconstruct one's life. Out of the new necessities of one's new life and new identity beyond the loss, there may be a need to develop new skills or characteristics. There will be moments of fear, guilt or apprehension, doubting whether you need to or can even move on after all the pain you feel today. Thank God for the hope that faith brings is us for such crossroads of life. Unfortunately, the pain of grief and loss is one experience each of us must some day undergo at one time or another. There is a motivational speaker, Les Brown, who says that if the messenger of doom has not visited with you, he may be knocking at your door in a little while or in the future. It is therefore important that we support those that are grieving today because tomorrow may be our turn.

Grieving the Loss of Broken Relationships

As we grow from one stage of life to the next; from childhood to adolescence; adolescence to young adulthood and finally into our fading declining stage, we develop all kinds of relationships. There are those we played with during our developing years, experimenting on anything and everything that captured our imagination. There will be those who have been there in different seasons of life, stayed beside us when we were celebrating and enjoying a good life. Then there are those who left and abandoned us when things changed for the worse. And finally there are those that kept vigil beside us when our lives were crashed and almost destroyed by one tragedy or another, like death in a family, getting caught up with criminal events and jail terms. There are those who keep in touch after circumstances cause us to move away from one location to another looking for greener pastures that never materialized.

Among those relationships, some will develop into intimate friendships – our best friends who know almost everything about us. We develop a deep sense of trust and confidence in them that we are occasionally able even to process our thoughts, dreams and aspirations openly with them, knowing that they accept us for who we are, loving us unconditionally. Some of these friendships eventually pave a way for courtship and future marriage. We even get our mutual families involved slowly, blissfully trusting things to keep moving to the right direction.

One party in these relationships might maintain dual relationships outside of the original setup. For one reason or another, they break lose and chose to move on, to the utter shock of the other person who all along never saw it coming and busy planning for a bigger future. Perhaps they were even engaged and way deep into wedding arrangements. The jilted lover gets caught up in total disbelief and denial while the other person moves fast and far away.

75

This happens often and the damage to the abandoned person can have long lasting damage, at times totally incapacitating the wounded one to such an extent that they can never trust anyone else in the future. Some such people who had started visualizing themselves in a marriage with the other person, have been known shut themselves off to marriage for the rest of their lives. Some develop a very permanent and negative dislike for the opposite sex, even within their families. Some however, gradually recover from the shock, but in a hurry to make it up to themselves might end up hooking themselves urgently just to anyone who comes along, without finding out if they are compatible. Some carry the blame of the broken relationships so heavily and unknowingly expose themselves to future abuse as they do anything to earn the love of whoever comes into their lives next.

Broken relationships have also been known to exist between parents and children. Where children have been sexually molested or abused by parents or other relatives, a permanent damage takes place to the extent that when they grow up and leave home they want nothing to do with their abusive parents ever again. I have had painful encounters with lonely patients who when asked if their parents have visited them will say they have had no contact with them for many years since they left home. I vividly remember a young woman in her early twenties, admitted with exhaustion and fatigue because of working double shifts for years. Alone and struggling to make a better life for herself, working and schooling, she just crashed. She had no idea where her parents were for the last seven years since she left home, living with boyfriends, finally hoping to marry her current one. She had no contact with her siblings either because her brothers also sexually abused her together with their father. I felt a sense of deep pain and desperation in her heart trying to survive alone and wanting nothing to do with her family of origin. This was too painful to comprehend and imagine what goes on in her mind when she breaks up with any of her boyfriends who might also just misuse her knowing she has no one else to turn to or even to protect her.

Looking at all this and aware that there are many other forms of broken relationships, I am quickly comforted by the remembrance that the one relationship that is secure, unconditional and free is our relationship with God our creator, Jesus our Savior and Holy Spirit our Comforter. The only time that this relationship is broken is when we turn away, look to and trust other men and women for our help and walk away from God. Having gone through a painful divorce myself after 30 years of marriage, I can empathize with anyone struggling and healing from a broken relationship. In my life, I did everything I could or knew how to save my marriage but had to painfully face the reality that even after giving it the best part of my life, my youth and my best intellect, it was not working for me. At that point, it was my long time relationship with Christ and the support of my family of origin, my own children and a few faithful Christian prayerful friends who helped me keep looking up to God for His sustaining grace through a very painful phase of my life.

The impact of broken relationships can be so devastating that some people never recover from it but end up in self destructive habits like alcohol, drugs and substance abuse and dependency in an effort to soothe their heartache. It matters how well grounded one is in their faith and who the cornerstone of their survival in life is. Paul said that while we may be crashed and tortured from all sides, yet if we remain in Christ we are not totally destroyed.

The Loss of Physical Ability

For as long as one is healthy, agile and able to do all the normal things that are relevant to one's age, desire and ability, it is hard to imagine the kind and depth of grief experienced by people when all the above is suddenly or gradually taken away either by illness, accidents or even mental conditions that steal the will to live and perform. At the peak of one's life, we take so much for granted that we can run, walk, sit or stand, sleep, eat, drink and swallow automatically. The fact that we can even blink, open or close our eyes as we choose without even giving it a thought, is actually a miracle.

But as you look around you in the community, in your family, at church, in your place of work or wherever else you interact with people, you start to notice people who are incapacitated in many ways. They face all kinds of challenges and can barely perform most of the things you do for yourself and others automatically. If you are anywhere in the medical field, in hospitals in any of the many disciplines that are involved in patient care of one kind or another, you will begin to notice and appreciate many of the very minute or simple things that the sick can no longer do on their own. Some are on ventilators and tubes of all kinds that are either breathing for them or literary sustaining their lives. How many times do we stop to thank God that we can breath the God-given fresh air, see the beauty of His creation, smell the roses and everything good, feel the taste of what we are eating or drinking, be able to void on our own and do a million and one things that millions can not do?

Diseases like cancer of the throat make it very hard to swallow, colon cancer results in all kinds of complications and some people end up with colostomy bag through which they void, some for the rest of their lives. Others have tubes inserted in their throat and can no longer speak audibly like you and me. Many have lost different limbs and other organs in accidents or major illnesses and have to be fitted with artificial limbs as a result of which their physical activities are greatly reduced or altered. There are numerous other changes in people's lives for me to list in this document.

As I reflect on all the above, and from my interactions with people in many of these categories, I cannot even start to imagine or describe the grief that must accompany most of these experiences by people who have been able bodied and very active in their lives. Some must now depend on family and friends for survival. Others end up in mental institutions and other medical facilities where they can be cared for. I have listened to the saddest and heart rending stories from many patients who wish their lives could turn around even a little. I have gotten to a point in life when I am conscious of how blessed I am that I can swallow food and water as I desire. Having been completely grounded and bed-ridden for months after a major back surgery, I thank God every waking moment, and remember to pray for those that have to live under such conditions for much longer. I am constantly reminding myself and others never to take anything for granted because the absence of these abilities has resulted in great grief for millions of people.

As a chronic pain advocate, I am aware of those that can no longer take care of their families as a result of these debilitating aches and pains, especially when they are ridiculed as just fussing or being too sensitive to pain. I know the deep grief of a father whose life has been totally altered by an incapacitating back pain that means he can no longer play soccer or any games with a teenage son he and his wife prayed for, for over ten years. This and many other parents in his boat will do or give anything in life to be able to play or do even the simplest things with their children. Yet those who can are not even aware of these gifts.

There are millions of couples who grieve throughout their lives that for one reason or another, they cannot bear children and some are not even physically able to adopt those that have no parents. There are all kinds of physical disabilities endured by millions everywhere that impact people's lives painfully and cause great physical and emotional grief. The sad thing is that often times these people do not get the support and sympathy they deserve to ease their pain. Many a times, we even react ignorantly and hurt them even more.

I had a humbling experience listening to a lady friend of mine who had all her life wanted to get married and have many children of her own. But for many different reasons and broken relationships, she never got married until the age of 54. She narrated many incidents when in the company of her different friends of both gender, she was made to feel less of a woman because she did not have any children. Without knowing her deep desire to have children, some went as far as to assume and tell her that she was too self-centered and did not want children. Unaware of what was going on in her life, a man colleague shared with another man friend that his wife was now expecting a baby and beginning to feel like a "real" woman. My friend wept as she narrated this incident, trying to help me understand the many women out there grieving for unfulfilled dreams. But instead of receiving sympathy and understanding, they felt judged and condemned for reasons beyond their control. Her sadness, and I guess of many others like her, was that many things were usually assumed about them and people were not even bothered to find out why they were who they were, and the fact there may be many unknown and unspoken reasons why they had no children of their own. After that I also remembered a young man who had shared with me the pain of letting go of a girl he had courted and dated for many years, to a point where they were beginning to consider the possibility of marriage. Unfortunately the girl got involved with one of their common friend and became pregnant even though they never got married. This young man, being a strong believer in the sanctity of marriage and God's part in the family, was so determined to pray and wait for a God fearing wife who would do ministry with him in the future, God willing. He too shared the many times people challenged him about his choice to wait or go it slow in the process of looking for a God fearing future wife. In the effort of self preservation and protection from a repeated broken heart, he did not want to rush into a serious relationship to please others, unless he felt comfortable to do so. He too was grieving the loss of his broken relationship, but there being no visible "death' to those around him, he received very little meaningful support and encouragement to believe in the future or sympathy for what he had lost. This continues to show how we as a society, even among believers, are often unduly ignorant of what others might be going through or why they are where or who they are in life. I am more and more sensitized to being less judgmental and assuming, but more tolerant of other people around me.

I also got a rude awakening as I listened to a young man who had battled cancer for over five years from his early teens. He talked of losing all his hair after the chemotherapy treatment for his cancer. For a vibrant young man who had lots of beautiful and healthy hair to style as he wanted, this was a big blow to his image and self esteem.

Ashamed of his bold head, he started wearing base ball caps and different kinds of hats everywhere he went. Without knowing his story, many people made jokes about it. In some places, he was forced to remove his hat before he could be attended to. Initially he would shyly explain why he was wearing the caps or hats but in some cases some people would adamantly tell him that it was not their problem but rules had to be obeyed. He talked of other children, school and classmates laughing at and making dirty jokes at him. He experienced great frustrations because of the many activities he could not participate in due to his sickness and constant body aches and pains. Part or the challenging reality was that cancer was mostly assumed to be a grown-ups disease just like heart, kidney, liver etc diseases. The sad truth is that illnesses do not discriminate between the young and the old but will attack anyone. This meant that most people do not know how to deal with or handle young children and young adults dealing with these diseases. The result is that they end up feeling out of place, neglected or even misunderstood. I know this for a fact because I attend to, counsel and minister at cancer survivors' camps organized by the cancer center at the hospital where I work. The participants range between very young and very senior adults and there are no special guidelines or strategies of catering for the younger ones with issues of self image and chances of their life span being cut short by cancer. This is what causes the isolation and a sense of loneliness for them in many places and situations.

These are just a few illustrations of many other categories of people dealing with equally painful grief but receiving very little sympathy and support most critical for their own healing. I believe it is time we spread word around for everyone to be more sensitive, understanding and caring for people who may appear odd in our midst yet saying nothing about themselves. I see the need for us to be more open to learning from others and being more tolerant and keen to learn why they appear and behave different.

When we think in terms of grief experienced under different situations, then we will be extra careful and considerate, be more prone to offer help as often as we can in order to take away some of their grief. We will remember to emotionally put ourselves in their shoes and think what they may be going through in order to be more innovative and creative in the ways we offer help without making them feel belittled or blamed for their fate. The reality is that what affects us physically has a great deal to do with our emotional and spiritual wellbeing as well. There is an increasing need for those dealing with any physical disability to be given grief support alongside other people undergoing various lose in life.

8

Pastoral Care To The Dying Children And Their Families

One of the most traumatic experiences is when families receive diagnosis of a terminal illness in a child of any age. The devastation results from the fact that we always view children as the best hope and assurance of our future generations. Many would wish they could swap places with the sick child to give them a chance in life. It brings a feeling of family roots being shaken up or pulled out of their very existence. They feel cheated by life and this may result in deep anger and grief.

Having one's child diagnosed with a terminal illness must be the hardest news for any parent or family. In an effort to protect and care for the dying child, people often hide the truth and the details from this child until too late. While this may be seen as a method of care for this child, it often leaves them translating it negatively, especially if they are a little old enough to reason and put two and two together in their experiences. The reality is that they are the ones who are hurting and experiencing all the body changes and decline of various vital organs as the disease advances.

I got exposed to this kind of experience as I walked along with close friends whose only daughter died of cancer at 6 years. This was my little friend Vivian who taught us a great deal through her fight with cancer. I knew this beautiful and happy spirited child from birth and saw her struggle first with diabetes from ages three and a cancer diagnosis a year later. She went through very sickly episodes of chemo and radiation with great support and loving care from both parents who would do practically anything to restore her health. While she loved them back in a very special way and reached out to all her family and friends, she underwent so many drastic changes in her brief journey on earth than any child should ever experience. While nobody wanted to discuss death and dying with or around her, her language, behaviors and interactions with people gradually told us she knew what was happening. She talked a lot about heaven and constantly hugged and assured her parents and friends that she deeply loved them. She gradually started telling her parents that "I *don't belong here and I want to go home*". As her cancer advanced and the effects of chemotherapy and radiation started taking its toll on her, she started distancing herself and would be found in her room quietly crying alone. At times she experienced feelings of loneliness and isolation since she no longer had the strength to play much with her friends or go to school.

Having experienced such statements and reactions from many terminally ill patients during my hospice work or at the critical care units at the hospital, I shared with the parents that she was caringly saying her goodbyes. I suggested to them that they need to emotionally step behind her, listen more keenly and allow her to lead them. She passed away peacefully in her sleep one afternoon less than three weeks thereafter. It was then that the grieving parents would share how finally her language turned into words of farewell with her assuring them she loved Jesus and would be going home with angels to heaven. At one point with many of her family gathered together in one home,

Vivian insisted in anointing everyone present with oil and took offence at those who declined.

The Sunday before she died, Vivian wanted to sing a song and refused help from her mother except that of holding her hand as she sang at her church. This ended up being her farewell to her church family and friends and knowing how sick Vivian was, there was no dry eye at the end of her song.

My little friend Vivian, who had also become like my adopted granddaughter, became a teacher in matters of death and dying to so many of us who walked alongside her in her last days here on earth. She sensitized me and many others of the need to listen and pay attention as the sick children share their innermost feelings which may include the fears of "why me and why now" or other needs. In their care for us and feeling that we are too vulnerable as parents and families to handle their pain and dying, they may not be very direct about it, but may even draw indicative pictures of angels in flight towards heaven, etc like my little friend Vivian did. As pastors and chaplains, we need to help the dying child and family remain open, honest and connected to each other at all times as best as is humanly possible. We can help the family understand the need to help the child remain connected also with her friends and peers to provide some form of continuity and support leveled to her age and mindset. This can be done via video tapes or by inviting their friends home to play simple games as long as the sick child is able and comfortable to do so. This is in line with what I have always found necessary and helpful when dealing with HIV/AIDS patients. Let us work towards "*Adding Life into every day they live*" instead of longing for more days that may never come. Chaplains and the clergy can also mediate between the family and the sick child by keenly listening to both parties and giving spiritual support and the hope of seeing each other again in heaven if either of them should die.

The greatest need is towards the dying moment because while there is every indication that this child is fast declining and dying, it is never easy to let go when the time comes. There may be moments of deep anger, shock and emotional outburst not just against those around, but also against God. Let us avoid comments like *"I understand"*. We really cannot understand another person's grief since grief is very personal and its intensity often dependent on the relationship between the deceased and the grieving person. As much as we know that the grieving person or family are believers comments like *"Your beloved is now in a better place in heaven with God"* may easily hurt a grieving person who was not ready to let go and who may even be angry with the deceased for leaving them alone. I am constantly reminded that some of the words I might say intending to console some grieving person may actually be more hurting than helpful. It is therefore important to be very observant of every reaction from the grieving persons, both verbal and non-verbal. The best one can do is be present and attentive, listen and allow them to express their feelings and emotions. We need to allow them to deal with their grief the way they feel like, without judging them. This may include screaming, rolling themselves on the floor, hitting walls, crying and laughing almost all at the same time Some end up telling jokes or stories about their loved ones even to the extent of what they think the deceased is doing or saying wherever they are at that time after death. The best we can do at such times is being present and attentive to ensure they are safe as they process their grief at that initial stage. At times, being silently present and offering tissue paper, water etc may be the greatest ministry moment than saying unnecessary words that leave heartache than help. After the funeral and the supporting crowds have subsided, continued pastoral visits will be helpful as grief and loss finally hits home with the vivid absence of their child or other loved one. Find out from them how best you can be of help. Drop a sympathy card or other little messages assuring them that you still care and continue to be available for them as best as the Lord leads you, especially if you are their pastor. It is well known that *"Grief Shared helps bond even strangers"*. Your visits or calls will help reduce feelings of loneliness and isolation for the family. It is also very important that while we minister and support the grieving parents, we do not overlook or forget the siblings to the departed child, whether they were younger or older than them. The death will definitely impact their lives in different ways, some of which might never be spoken of or addressed yet they might affect their interpersonal relationships or even school performance. We need to include them and check out how best to help the grieving family. Allow and encourage them to share their feelings of loss and what they need to be able to continue as best as possible. School, classmates, church families and extended families can provide good and much needed support at such times. But allow the children to guide you on how best to help them without imposing everything on them. The same goes for living grandparents who may even be angry at God and everyone as to why their grandchild, their future hope, should die leaving them behind with lives and bodies that are barely functioning. There may also be other close relatives like cousins who grew up with the deceased child or aunties/uncles who were closely involved with his/her growing up and can barely cope with the loss.

9

CHILDREN DEALING WITH
GRIEF & BEREAVEMENT

General statistics have shown that before the age 18 years, one in 20 children will have undergone the loss of one parent. More often than not, the children who lose a parent are at greater risk of depression, withdrawal, struggle with poor self esteem, sexual experimentation, behavior problems, anxiety, etc. These children fall in a category that may require some extra kind of understanding from the family and the community at large. When there is a loss in the family or community, children's grief is often overlooked or disregarded unintentionally. There is great focus on the adults and we often forget that they too are affected and grieving for different reasons, some of which they may never be able to express. The reality is that children grieve even when they do not have the coping mechanisms like adults. They often struggle with sadness, anger, guilt, insecurity and anxiety. The age of every child determines how best they understand death. The preschool ones think death is temporary and the dead loved one will come back later. Those 5 to 9 years of age see death as a separation with their beloved deceased person.

From 9 or 10 years, they slowly begin to understand the finality of death. While they may not fully understand the finality and concept of death and its aftermath, and cannot clearly explain what is going on in their minds, they are equally affected and at a loss like everyone else in the family. Perhaps they are even more deeply impacted by the loss than we may ever know. They may not only be trying to handle and learn to accept the finality of death, but also understand that it is irreversible and dead people function differently from the living. Some may not be at an age of understanding any of the above but are equally confused and frustrated. If proper care and attention is not paid to them during their grieving period, some learn to subdue and hide their feelings and sometimes anger at the dead person who may be a parent, a grandparent, a sibling or a close family member or friend who had a special place in their lives and heart. Many times, these emotions have been known to explode in the most unexpected places and times, even against the wrong people who perhaps had nothing to do with what happened and don't even know anything about it. Unresolved grief can easily manifest itself in people's lives at different stages of life and even be destructive. It is therefore important that while grief and bereavement support is given to the adults in the family, children and young adults are also involved and invited to participate even in the care and eventually funeral arrangements to facilitate for their goodbyes as well as coming to an appropriate closure with the death of their loved one.. Let them freely share their feelings and emotions in an environment that nurtures their healing and coping with death in the future. This also gradually introduces them to their own mortality and encourages them to live meaningful lives. It paves forums of facing and discussing matters of life and death as well as some inevitable crucial stages and crossroads of life that everyone will have to face in the journey of life. Their questions should be kindly and patiently answered and not ridiculed or belittled.

At such moments, children may also be dealing with spiritual issues of where God is in all these issues. Based on what they have heard along the way in adult conversations, some will be heard asking why God would allow the death of their loved ones, especially a parent/grandparent/guardian or a beloved sibling or friend who has meant much to them. As they grow and understand better, feeling embraced and encouraged to grieve in their own way, they become supportive and more accommodating of the grieving adults around them. The hard truth is that death colors every moment of every day for the child when death strikes any family or friend, both at home and school. Adults and parents therefore need to patiently explain and guide them through grief as best as possible in simple clear language.

It is even worse when their emotions and feelings are disregarded, ignored or not acknowledged by those around them. A little later a child may be very angry as reality hits home, as to why a parent would die and leave them alone. Worse still is in the case of an adolescent who will often translate a parent's death as an act of abandonment. They might even blame them for dying of diseases caused by unhealthy habits like cigarette smoking and lung cancer, HIV/AIDS etc. Even in the case of a terminal illness, children might translate it as quitting the battle without considering them.

I had such an encounter with a 17 year old young man brought to the emergency room after an attempted suicide and ending up in one of the critical care units where I was in charge of pastoral care needs. When he was finally revived and stabilized, he was angry with practically everyone who went to his room, demanding that he should have been left to die. I visited him daily, told him I was just checking if he needed help, which he declined, until the fourth day when he burst out in painful tears amidst sobs. I sat quietly with him until he calmed down and was willing to tell me about himself and the attempted suicide. After several days of trying to connect with him, he burst out angrily that his single mother, his only hope and friend, fully aware that nobody else really cared about him should not have died leaving him at the mercy of his very old grandparents who were too old to understand and guide him through his adolescent developmental years. He knew they loved him but they just could not take care of him. He felt they too needed care from someone, but not an added burden of caring for him. He wept and sobbed for a long time and all I could do was sit quietly beside him, praying silently with my hand on his shoulder.

In helping the grieving child, the clergy and pastoral caregivers need to be down to earth with them, be attentive and listen. Children experience lots of different losses in each death of a loved one. In a parent's death, they grieve the loss of their identity, their close friends, familiar living environment when this brings a necessity for them to go live with their grandparents or other relatives. Some start a whole new way of life in foster homes. They need very sensitive support and permission to be themselves in their grief.

There may be periods of poor school performances, bad dreams and nightmares, explosion of bad or violent behaviors confusion about God and heaven etc. Their behaviors may at times be very unpredictable and they need understanding rather than blame and judgment. They need greater compassion, understanding, honesty and love from those around them especially during this critical transition that dramatically affects their lives. The adults also need to be consistent and good in guiding them in their healing process. Good listening and gentle communication helps them to know that grief is natural. Let us not hide away the sorrow, tears and brokenness even as we minister to people, bearing in mind that whatever our roles, we are first and foremost human beings with feelings and emotions like everyone else. This allows others to be natural in their grieving process without striving and struggling to impress us or others around them at these crucial moments.

It is important too, that adults avoid over-shielding children from attending funerals as that deprives them of opportunities to say their good byes, coming to terms with the finality of death and absence of their loved ones from that time forth. Bearing in mind that death is a definite and inevitable part of every human being, it is important that children are taught gradually as they grow in their understanding, etc, what happens at death, funerals or burials. Many people view this negatively, but it is important to induct children into the real matters of life which helps them to handle their grief appropriately even as adults. It also makes it easier for the parents in guiding their children to participate in family grief, embrace whoever has died, tell their stories or even write letters to the deceased as a rite of passage. It also helps the community to see the continuity of life and future even in the loss of a parent or grandparent. It is equally important to offer group support to children under the guidance and close watch of adults and clergy. Watch out too for destructive anger, serious behavior changes, intense withdrawal episodes etc, and address these issues and challenges sensitively, compassionately and without judging them. It may be wise to refer children and families to professional counselors as needs arise. It is increasingly important for people to talk about death and dying constantly to educate and create a forum where they can express and share their fears, sadness, anger, etc. It is critical that support continues for the grieving children without necessarily pushing them too fast out of it. Depending on the relationship the child had with the deceased, grief may linger on beyond the funeral and other rituals that may follow. It is at that point that some children will start asking all kinds of unanswered questions popping up from different situations around them. It is very important to remember too that from this time forth, children who have experienced grief in the loss of a loved one might suddenly become fearful of more losses whenever another loved one falls sick or is injured. The surviving parent, siblings or other relatives and friends need to be patient, loving and compassionate in comforting them with assurance that all will be well. The child has reasons to doubt such words and so it is everyone's responsibility to assure them in a realistic way that the sick person could either get better or die. The most important thing is to be forthright and truthful in a language and method that is clear and appropriate to their level of understanding. Overprotecting the children and hiding the truth is not helpful and not only complicates their grieving process, but also their growth and development process. Let the surviving parent of the grieving child maintain daily routines like bed-time, meal-time and scheduled activities and games. Make an effort to hug, hold or cuddle the child as often as possible. Be patient and tolerant with them when they exhibit some regressive behaviors like thumb sucking or wetting their beds even though they had already stopped that. Encourage them to express their feelings and emotions in a healthy way as you share your own in an open and honest way with them. As you do this, you are telling them that their feelings are normal and genuine, so they do not need to be ashamed of them. When you do not have an answer for their questions, tell them in a simple and clear language that you simply don't have an answer, but sit with them and be really present to their emotional needs. Do not dodge their questions or confusion If the child unexpectedly explodes and acts in some unacceptable way, don't react in anger or punish them. Instead, address the behavior and slowly but carefully explore the feelings and thoughts.

10

Teenagers adn Grief – Helping Them To Cope

At every stage in life, grief can be unbearable, especially in the loss to death of a parent or a close guardian. It is even harder during the adolescent years when one is crossing from childhood to the turbulent years of young adulthood. The teenagers may experience the overwhelming loss of someone who helped shape their still fragile self identities. They may go through serious episodes of total confusion, anger, feelings of rejection and abandonment by a parent at a time when they need them most. These feelings about death will be part of their permanent history for ever. For lack of understanding, they may go into stages of questioning why their parent "gave in" and perhaps died of a disease that a friend's parent may have endured or survived like cancer etc. We have to remember that their own understanding is limited. Where a death has resulted from bad habits or lifestyle like alcohol, drugs and substance abuse, the anger and blame may be even worse. They translate it that their parent or elder sibling who was their anchor or support was not loving or caring enough to live for them. This anger also destroys trust for others in their lives. It may cause them to distance themselves in self protection and preservation from similar future heartache.

As the teens struggle with all these emotions or grief and bereavement, many things are likely to go wrong. The academic performance may suddenly drop as well as their morale or motivation. They lack focus, concentration and a sense of direction. The teen may struggle in his anger, feeling that if his life will ever improve or makes a meaning, it will have to be squarely dependent on him. For this reason, he or she might make drastic changes and completely drown themselves on a journey to achieve and live their dreams since there is now nobody else to do so. This is more so when the deceased parent was their favorite one. They may even go to the extent of emotionally and psychologically blocking out everyone else and simply withdrawing from everything and everyone for lack of trust on others.

Unfortunately, even through the season of grieving, the adolescent will still be undergoing the normal psychological, physiological, academic and all other pressures relevant to his age. They may already be undergoing pressure from all sides to "grow up" and facing the challenge of leaving the security of childhood and home, to face the wide unknown world of challenges galore without the protection of the departed parent. The scary process of separation from parents, siblings and family may already have begun and rocked the boat of life. They are already anxious and fearful. Then suddenly their guide, their mentor and their point of reference suddenly dies. Whether the deceased parent has been sick for sometime or not, to a teenager, especially experiencing the death of a loved one for the very first time, this must appear sudden and unexpected.

With the death of a parent, the pressure is heightened as everyone starts calling upon the teenager to pull themselves up and learn to be a "good/strong" support for the surviving parent. They are quickly reminded that they are no longer children, yet on the other hand they are not fully acknowledged as adults. The may go through moments of overwhelming feelings and pressure from every side. Unless handled with loving care and compassionate understanding, this can be a dangerous time where suicide may become a contemplated option. They begin to hear comments like "You need to be a strong role model for your younger siblings and show them how to survive. You must grow up fast and carry on your father/mother's legacy". Contrary to this, the teenager is longing and wishing for the return of their newly deceased parent or elder sibling. They are not interested with carrying on with anybody's legacy. Often time, for lack of knowledge, many adults discourage teens from mourning or sharing their grief openly.

What the teenagers yearn for during their grief or bereavement is that adults be open, honest and loving so they can effectively help them learn both the joy and pain that comes from caring deeply for others. Feeling dazed and numb at the death of a loved one is a normal part of the teens' grieving process just as it is for everyone else. The numbness helps emotions to catch up and face the reality of their loss at a safe gradual pace that is comfortable and specific to each individual as always. The numbness also insulates them from hearing or experiencing too much too quickly of what they don't want to hear. It is wrong to assume that the grieving adolescent has more than enough friends or family support for this transition and therefore leave them out when caring for their grieving parents or younger siblings. This only fuels the anger and feelings of rejection and needs to be addressed and attended to before it is too late. These are social expectations and assumptions that we all need to be sensitive to or careful with.

The teenagers are often pushed into roles of care for the surviving parents and younger siblings (even surviving grandparents) without permission, encouragement or space to mourn or grieve their own losses. Unless their teenage friends have undergone personal losses and grief, they will be of little or no support. Instead they might even ignore the subject of loss completely from their conversations because it makes them uneasy and they don't know how to handle it. Nobody needs to hear words or comments like "Since we cannot change this situation, you just need to grow up and move on with life as best as you can". Worse still is when a parent dies and the surviving family has to move into a smaller unfamiliar home or apartment on their own or with other family members. These may even be people they never related with closely or well and only God knows how they will survive. I have known international families from different cultures and other parts of the world who have lost a loved one, be it a parent, a spouse or one's child. The trauma that goes with this kind of a situation cannot be described in any adequate words. Their grief is multiplied many times over, as they organize finances, air tickets, disposing of their household goods, at times even those of sentimental value and personal memorabilia as they cannot afford to ship them back to their home country on top of the expensive air tickets for themselves and the remains of their loved one. I cannot even try to imagine the agony of two teenage children and their father, having lived in a foreign land for most of these children's lives now going back without their mother to help them settle back in their families and communities where they have not been for over 10 years. It must be even harder for the widower who must also find his way back home alone in tears and grief while he went abroad in search of education and a better life for his family, hoping to return home loaded with all the good things they all dreamt of together. This is what would truly be unfathomable grief and disorientation for each of them.

However, as time passes, those caring for the teens must watch out for the following symptoms and act before it is too late.

- Chronic depression, sleeplessness, restlessness and poor self esteem.

- Poor academic performance or lack of interest for school activities, even the ones they enjoyed before.

- Risk taking behaviors such as alcohol and drug abuse, fighting, rudeness, sexual experimentation, loss of appetite or sudden overeating.

- Denying pain and acting overly mature and "OK"

It may be necessary to look for school counselors, church groups or even a private grief therapist. Provide the grieving teenager with safe and nurturing outlets for this season of his life which he too cannot quite understand. Give them permission to grieve and vent as necessary. Be willing to stand by them as best and as closely as possible during their healing or reconstruction process. Teenagers cannot choose between grieving and not grieving. As you willingly, compassionately and lovingly walk with the adolescent through their grieving journey, you are giving the best gift ever. *The Gift of Yourself,* which may be the ultimate gift of healing for them. You will help alleviate feelings of abandonment, insecurity, low self esteem, shock and anger and give them a sense of relief and your much needed companionship.

While there are all kinds of support systems for the grieving students, there is a very special role for the teachers, school mates and classmates. School is in reality, a home away from home, especially because students spend three quarters of their waking time in the school communities. It can therefore be a place of refuge, offering a stabilizing environment where they can openly share their feelings of fear and anger without necessarily being ridiculed or asked to suddenly grow up and take care of others. It would help if you can earn their trust and be able to come down to whatever level they are in life, look them in the eye and tell them "I am here for you and willing to help you through your grief as best as I can . I know you and I can count on a few other teachers and students who feel for you and want to support you".

Your effectiveness as a school teacher or counselor will largely depend on how much you know and how current you are on the subject of death and dying. This is a topic that most of us would rather not get involved in unless it becomes a real necessity. It may also cause you to delve into your own life's journey to know when and how you dealt with death in your own family, and its impact on you, especially if you were still a child. This will better equip you to be a better help for grieving students. But this calls you to be intentional in how you relate with your students, taking every opportunity to reflect on matters of life and death. Occasions like the birth of a new baby in the family, the death of a grandparent, the death of a pet, or a friend will help open up conversations on this topic. Dr. Alan D. Wolfelt, Ph.D. calls these *"Teachable Moments"* and *"Created Moments"* of addressing issues of life and death as well as grief and bereavement. This also helps break up the barriers to discussing death. We need to help our children grow knowing the reality that when death strikes it is both natural and permanent. This knowledge will be an important pillar of support when they need it most and with no time to prepare.

Harder still is the unexpected death of a classmate that suddenly tells them that they too carry the potential to die young. In the healing/recovery process, you might encourage the students to make drawings or write letters give to the deceased student's parents. This will not only help the students in their grief process, but also the grieving family. At some point some students may need further counseling if their grief becomes complicated and prolonged. Consider wisely referring them to a professional counselor with vast experience in counseling traumatized children and students.

- Be a good observer in order to detect behavioral and personality changes that might need quick intervention.

- Be patient. The teens may appear confused or even disoriented.

- Be honest and don't lie to them about death Let them know its finality and permanence

- Allow them to grieve at their own pace, individually or in groups if it will help them deal with their loss of a common friend.

11

Un-Acknowledged Grief or Non-Bereavement Losses.

Just as much as God is no respecter of persons, death has a definite date with everyone born of woman and man. The bible tells us that God sends rain to everyone on the earth, both rich and poor. Grief is another thing in life that strikes whoever loses a loved one to death. Regardless of the kind of life they led, everyone's death is likely to bring grief and pain to somebody somewhere. It may be a parent or family whose son or daughter has killed another person, intentionally or accidentally and ended up executed or committed to serve a life sentence for their crime. The family of the victim and the family of the criminal will both face issues of grief. Needless to say, the victim's family will be dealing with deep anger and loss. As much as is possible, they will receive grief and other support from family and friends, known and even unknown sympathizers. And when such a case is exposed to the public through media covering, they will receive emotional, spiritual, moral and even material support from near and far away On the contrary, the family of the accused criminal, however good they may be in their community, will more often than not experience condemnation, isolation, resentment and rejection from everyone around them. Because of the anger that goes with this, they will probably receive very little sympathy or consolation for their own loss. They will also not feel comfortable grieving their loss openly. I can only imagine any parent or child going through this kind of grief.

Another un-acknowledged grief would result from the family of one who kills their parent(s) or sibling(s) and is subsequently sentenced to death. The immediate family will have a double tragedy because not only have they lost the initial murdered victim, but they will end up losing the second family member who did the killing. In the case of one who kills their parent(s), any surviving siblings will go through the untold agony of dealing with the loss of their parents and eventually a sibling either to execution or to prison for life. Yes they will be angry at the loss of their parent(s) and perhaps receive emotional and other support for their loss, but people will find it hard to console them for losing their sibling too. Their anger too, may inhibit them from dealing with their grief in a healthy way. Worse still is the grief of any living grandparents of such a child who painfully not only lose their own child but subsequently their grandchild. This kind of grief has the potential to bring them to an early death. These are some of the unresolved family dynamics that end up exploding in the most unexpected consequences, places and times.

Just as much as life is diverse in every respect, so are there as many reasons for grief as you can ever imagine. Think of a parent whose child young or adult has committed murder or other serious crimes that commits him to prison for life without parole, after several years of waiting or even trying to fight for his life. It has often been the case that in such instances, especially where the serious crime is obvious that almost everyone gives up on the person in question. But the parents will hang in there with their son or daughter until the final verdict is given. They will then enter into their own emotional prison of grieving and mourning their child behind their own home prison doors. The sad reality is that while those whose child is dead and buried will have some form of closure, mourn and receive grief support, these parents receive little or no support or sympathy for their loss. This loss also carries more anger and guilt at times for what their child will have done. I have had an encounter with such parents who were looking for a support group that would be willing to walk with them. Apparently, there are support groups for those whose children are in prisons but very rarely for such parents as described above. The closest support one might find for them is if their pastors or church are kind and understanding enough to help them at least through the initial phase of a grief which they must endure for the rest of their lives.

A young teenage girl may become pregnant and decide to abort the baby to conceal the event in fear of the immediate consequences from parents or looking at the long term responsibility for which she is not prepared. She is mostly unaware of the after effects and naively assumes that life will go back to normal immediately. Unfortunately, a few days later she is not only consumed with guilt, but also by a deep sense of unexplainable grief and sadness. She may try all she can to look and play well as always, but this can become an unacknowledged secret grief that could lead into depression and numerous other disorders. It may haunt her any time she sees a child known to have been born around the same time she aborted her own.

The same scenario may involve a woman who for many reasons, from financial, complicated family dynamics etc. which she feels are not conducive to having a baby or more children, decides to go through an abortion. Without justifying abortion, the reality is that at some point in her life sooner or later, she will have to face the reality of her emotions, loss, grief and painful absence of a baby that she never saw or held in her hands. This too may become an unending grief, especially if later in life any of the above categories of women decide to have a baby, but cannot due to complications from the abortion. If nobody knows about this, she will for ever be judged and even laughed at for her "self-induced" barrenness.

Miscarriages and still births are other deaths that result in deep grief but often very little emotional support is given to the grieving parents. Many people assume that since the pregnancy was only a few weeks or months old it's no big deal. And so it is, that while a mother & father who lost an infant or toddler is surrounded by much love, support and sympathy from family and friends, this other family fades into the cracks to grieve their loss alone or with only a brief support.

Yet again, they too will often remember their loss at the sight of a child born around the same time theirs own baby would have been born. But because of the reactions of those around them, often resulting from the common discomfort of dealing with any form of death, they too will behave like all is well in public but weep alone at night or in secret places without sharing their pain and grief with anyone. They will have no little grave spots to visit and come to terms with their loss, and very rarely any pictures or memorials for the baby. Thank God for advanced grief support systems that are now helping make some memorial pictures, foot/hand prints of the little babies born too early to survive and even allowing such parents to spend some bonding time with their little babies beautifully dressed. Some of these parents have called for chaplains to do a memorial service for their little ones, praying for them and their families that God will sustain them in their journeys ahead. This also goes for full term babies who for one reason or other pass away.

The hardest part of my ministry in the Labor and Delivery units is watching a family that arrived in the delivery room with little baby clothes, cameras on the ready and baby's car seat, only to watch them carry everything back home but

without the long awaited baby. I watched helplessly at a couple who arrived at the ER as the wife was having serious abdominal aches. They were quickly told that they were in the process of losing a baby they never knew they were expecting in the first place. The baby was born and when the man was offered a chance to see his little baby son (the mother did not want to see the baby), he was heard telling the little baby to look out for his older brother who had died at the age of 7 a year earlier from a previous marriage. The explosion of his unresolved previous grief was because his ex-wife had full custody of their deceased son and so he had not attended the funeral. His un-acknowledged grief came as a shock to his grieving wife who knew nothing about it until then. Until that moment, his grieving wife said that while they both tried to rest and come to terms with their loss, she had heard him silently asking God "why me, why have you done this to me ***again.*** She said that all along she felt confused but was now able to understand and console her husband who was now handling double grief.

Rape, incest and increasingly sodomy victim must deal with one of the most painful grief and loss, where one cannot openly share or express their emotions and heartache.

The secret grief of having someone forcefully take complete charge/control of one's body must be one of the most painful experiences. This often results in self blame, condemnation and judgment and worse still potentially dangerous impact on any future relationships. Alongside the deep grief is also being blamed for the rape by those who get to know about it of what you did or did not do to bring it upon oneself. If the rape/sodomy victim gets married later and hides the incident from their spouse, this could have very adverse effects on their marriage. In some unfortunate cases, the victims have taken out of their anger by becoming abusers themselves. Grieving such pain in secrecy has deprived millions of victims healing support and sympathy because of their fear of being hurt further by people's reactions. The worst is in cases of incest where a father abuses a daughter, and when the daughter reports this to the mother or guardian, the whole matter is hushed up as if it never happened. The victim is not only threatened by the abuser never to tell anyone or face dire consequences including death, but receives similar treatment from her mother. For some such victims, their deep secret grief has become their close companion till death.

Worse still is the grief experienced by a couple expecting their first child only to lose it to a miscarriage or a still birth because of one complication or another. The saddest part is that from the first time they become aware of their expected baby, their mindset completely changes to adapt to their new roles. They start thinking of names, anticipating the gender of the baby and many other fantasies as to how their baby would look like, and all the things they would do together as a family as he grew up. Some start arranging the baby's room, buying baby clothes and books. Then suddenly there is a miscarriage or the baby with only a few more weeks to go is born dead or dies in the birthing process. The agony that these parents undergo is unexplainable and their grief inconsolable. The same painful experiences go for grandparents who had excitedly awaited their grand child with great anticipation. My ministry to such families as the chaplain for a hospital's labor and delivery unit is the hardest. As a mother myself, I can never find appropriate words to address their sorrow as the tiny little babies are brought to the mother to hold and cuddle before they leave the hospital. The thought of a mother who came to deliver her baby, bringing the dainty blue or pink baby clothes plus a new baby's car seat, but now going back home alone in tears is the most heartbreaking scenario. The unfortunate thing is that many people have no clue how deep the pain of such parents must be. Most people assume that since the miscarried or still born baby had not lived among them, she or he will not be missed as much as a two or ten years old baby.

The reality is quite on the contrary as they leave a deep vacuum that even their future babies cannot fill.

These parents might not even have a grave spot to visit in the future for their baby. They may have photos taken before the infant's body is left at the hospital for burial. In some cases of miscarriage only a few weeks into the pregnancy, there will be no chance to hold the baby at all and they will always miss that bonding moment. It may take them a great many months and years to come to terms with that loss.

Job losses and loss of one's identity and livelihood have increasingly become a major and traumatic challenge to many individuals. Nobody is exempted, regardless of age, career path of social status. Gone are the days when one would almost automatically, if so desired, expect or hope to work towards planned retirement in careers like teaching, management and administration, etc. In the past, with adequate education, training, self-discipline and good work ethics, one could more easily chart one's career path, possible or anticipated promotions, etc. one could even at times be able to forecast what retirement will be like financially etc. Unfortunately, the work life and environment have drastically changed and very few people can comfortably achieve their retirement goals and expectations. It is not a surprise that a lot more elderly people continue working to earn their basic living long after their retirement age. Many such people silently grieve the loss of their retirement dreams of going on vacations, on cruises, doing things for and with their grandchildren, or simply affording a comfortable life without having to depend on their children or welfare handouts. As much as the companies and corporations are downsizing the workforce, so are families and individuals being forced to cut down their expenses in order to survive. The sad reality and grief is that people are now *surviving* instead of living.

In a nutshell, there is little or no job security assured to any employee. When you hear of an employee being laid off from work from as early as 40 years of age, with a young family, a mortgage and perhaps multiple healthcare issues in the family, you can only imagine the devastation and grief that this must bring to the entire family. The parents of this employee might have been dependent on them as their own health starts to fail and on the other hand might now be compelled by circumstances to start sharing their retirement savings to help raise their grandchildren. It is therefore only fair to say that the loss of a job can be a serious vicious cycle or traumatic experiences, not just to the employee and breadwinner, but to all other people dependent on him for one need or another. Feelings of anger and inadequacy lead to depression, withdrawal and grief over their losses. They may end up feeling compelled to make a lot of forced adjustments to their lifestyles.

12

Coping with Grief:

Picking up the Pieces of our Broken Lives

It is hard to think of where one begins on this topic considering the drastic and permanent changes that the death of a loved one brings in our lives, regardless of how young or old. It is even harder to know when the healing and coping with one's grief ever begins, bearing in mind that every day brings new waves of sadness, emptiness, anger, questions and a roller coaster of emotions. Part of the anger against others may be that perhaps they could have done something to save the life of the deceased. Again, Jesus gives us permission to weep when touched by the jugged splintered edges of grief, pain and sorrow as found in Martha and Mary at the death of Christ's friend and their brother, Lazarus. Christ has a tender heart that hurts with us. At our lowest and saddest moments, Christ sits with us, holds us and weeps with us. He grieves with us and compassionately comforts us in times of unbearable grief, sorrow and despair. Once again, we must remember that this phase too will be very personal and there are no set standards or length of time by which this must begin. With time and with God's understanding and help, you will survive this. He will help you forge a new relationship with the one who has gone ahead of you. Grief is part of the healing process.

The following are suggestions and guidelines from which different people can find help based on where they are with their kind of grief. I would encourage each of us to do what is best for them and their situations and therefore adjust these ideas to suit them. One's faith in God plays a major role of support and encouragement. It may be quiet prayer or meditation, religious services and ceremonies, or other activities at your place of worship. Do not push yourself too hard but be moderate with expectations upon self. There may be moments, however, when you might feel angry with God, even wonder where God was when this tragedy happened, even wondering whether He caused it, etc. The most encouraging thing at such a time is to remember that God is big enough to love and accept you as well as your anger. Be honest with God – He can handle it. One of the most consoling things to remember is that Jesus knows and understands the real pain of grief and loss. In Mark 15 verse 34 Jesus cried out to His Father just before he gave up His soul. "*My God, my God, why have you forsaken me*"? At that point on the cross when Christ took upon Him all our sins and transgressions, His father could not bear it and looked away from His son for a moment. He experienced the deep sorrow then and so fully understands our pain even when it is too deep or painful for us to express it.

In John 11:35 "Jesus Wept" when He was told that His good friend Lazarus had died. This way He gave us permission to weep when touched by the jugged, splintered edges of grief, pain and sorrow. It reminds us that Christ too has a tender heart and fully understands our heartache at a moment of grief. At our lowest and saddest moment, Christ sits with us, holds us and weeps with us. He grieves with us and comforts us in times of unbearable grief and despair. In John 11 verses 25-26,

Jesus said "He is the resurrection and the life so that those who believe in Him, even though they die like everyone else, yet they shall live again". It is most important that the grieving person acknowledges their grief and loss without trying to be heroic or unrealistically strong about it. In the loss of a child, a grieving father may plunge into excessive work to help cope with his pain while the mother felt a more intense need for him. If this reaction to grief is not checked and addressed it could very easily cause marital problems for two people who are both traumatized and broken. It is important that you be kind to yourself and allow yourself space and time to feel and process your pain and loss. Be honest and face your feelings of anger, guilt, jealousy etc. Many times, people who come forward for healing prayers are actually grieving for one thing or another. The intermittent feelings of grief should not be viewed necessarily as a set back in the grieving process. It is a reflection that the lives of others were important to you and that you are grieving their loss. Turn them into healing opportunities. One of the first signs of recovery is the ability to recognize and accept that a loss has occurred.

The grieving person must seek support from friends, family and clergy who are able to listen patiently and with understanding and eventually from a relevant support group. These must be patient and compassionate people who will support the grieving person without being judgmental at a time when they may very well be going in circles of confusion, desperation and even denial. If however, they do not seek help, families and friends must take initiative and reach out to offer help, even when at times it may be declined for some time. It is important to assure them that as and when they need it, you will be there for them. The griever prefers you to be real and do not pretend to be strong for them. Help or facilitate for them to talk about what happened and their relationship with the person who has died. They will for ever cherish your encouragement to talk to you about what matters to them most. But, if they are not ready or willing to talk, do not be offended. Bring up the topic and let them decide if they want to talk about it or not.

A grieving person needs friends who are willing to:

Cry with them	Have creative ideas for coping
Provide practical help	Encourage independence
Be genuine	Be present
Show up Even when it is awkward	Take initiative
Be a supportive friend not a Hero	Reminisce
Listen	- Pause
Be honest	Offer comfort
Be there over the Long Haul	Bo compassionate
Be in touch with their own feelings	Sit quietly with them
Help them feel loved and needed	Believe that they will make through their grief
Be a Helpful Resource	

Friends are quiet angels, who lift us to our feet when we are so overwhelmed and ready to quit. The simple word "imagine" is good for opening comfortable conversations, making the grieving person know that whatever they say will be taken seriously. Instead of saying "I understand" it is better to say something like "I can't even imagine what this has done to you and your family". Always remember that good taste and good timing, choice of words is crucial in your conversation with the grieving person. One of the most comforting things for a grieving person is when others tell their own personal stories of grief and loss. ***There are many things in life that can only be seen through eyes that have cried. (Oscar Romero) Like grief.*** How they miss their loved ones, what has helped them and how they remember them during special occasions, anniversaries, etc. toasting them or singing their favorite songs. This encourages other grievers to share their own heartache and reduces a sense of isolation and loneliness.

> *"The ability to communicate our emotions openly and clearly, whether happy or sad, is one of the most distinguished characteristics of being human and vulnerable like everyone else around you. It is less human to exclude from discussions those people who have been important in our lives. Recovery from loss is achieved by a series of small and correct choices made by the griever"* (By Russell Friedman, John W. James and the Grief Recovery Institute 2002-2006)

Journaling ones feelings and thoughts will also help release one's piled up emotions. Don't worry about the spellings, the grammar or the vocabulary at the time. Simply express your loneliness, fears, sadness, what you wish you had told your dearly departed, how you miss them etc. Gradually, you will come to a comfortable place of telling them

"Goodbye, go in peace. I'll be Okay till we meet again." Draw from your own personal coping strength, consistent to you personally. Readjusting to new circumstances minus your departed loved one will not be an overnight thing. As mentioned over and over, grief is very personal. How ironic it is that we push away or fend off what is a life given condition – the need to mourn. (Alan D. Wolfelt) The way you cope is very different from everyone else. Do whatever suits you to ease your pain and grief. You can write, sing, talk to someone, paint, clean house, and listen to your favorite music that soothes your heartache or comforts you the best. "Your pain/ grief is the breaking point of the shell that encloses your own understanding". (Kahil Gibran).

It may be helpful to plan ahead the best way to deal with any kind of holiday or anniversary to ensure that they do not bring any undue heartache or new spells of grief. Aspire to do things that will ease these emotions and help with the healing and survival process without your loved one. The grieving person must be respected, understood and not be judged and made to feel guilty for the choices they will make at this time. It is wisdom to give them time to process their losses at their own pace without imposing ourselves on them of infringing on their privacy or space and time. While there is no set time frame for grieving and recovering from their losses, they will gradually start coping and adjusting to what is around them. But it is also important to watch out for prolonged grief that turns into depression. Some signs may be self-criticism, intense or protracted grief, neglect of one's appearance, bouts of crying etc. It is wise to seek help before this turns into "Post Traumatic Stress Disorder (PTSD)" It is very important to take good care of oneself, to help the body, mind and spirit recover. Eat regularly your favorite foods, exercise and get enough rest and relax. Get a massage; learn to play a new music instrument. Sit out on the porch in a rocking chair for a while, visit a beautiful garden and stop to smell the roses. Learn to laugh, laugh, and laugh!! Treat yourself to a hot bath and take naps whenever you can. See your physician for any health conditions you may have neglected while you concentrated on caring for your loved one now gone out of your life. Avoid alcohol or using other drugs as these may slow your recovery and even cause you new problems.

May I bring out here other aspects of losses in life which equally become magnified in holiday seasons. Your loved one may still be alive but very sick. They may also have undergone major life changing events that have drastically reduced the extent of their activities like traveling, hiking, seasonal sports like skiing, boat riding and various other games. Perhaps you have always taken part in some regular challenge events together in the past but this seems to have come to an end for your companion and you don't feel like doing it alone. This brings in some amount of grief that often goes un-noticed.

Find a way of addressing this between the two of you in order to process your feelings. This will help you avoid angry feelings which if not dealt with might explode in the wrong places and at the wrong times. Perhaps your spouse might actually still want you to go ahead and participate as you always did together since you are still able to. This enhances your relationship and care for each other as necessary and retains some amount of "normal" feelings.

Change some old routines or traditions if you think this will ease your journey through grief, like meal times or where you sat with your loved one in church. Keep in the company of people who will understand and allow you to be yourself and share your feelings and experiences as necessary. Avoid moving or changing jobs in the first year in order to keep your roots and some sense of security and continuity. As much as you can, make provisions for some quiet time alone to remember your loved one, talk to them and deal with your personal intense feelings, meditation or silent walk. You might also choose to occupy your mind and time with activities and hobbies, volunteering yourself, travel, caring for a new pet, help others in their own bereavement. Take adult education classes etc. Help others understand what is going on within and realize that they too are processing their grief especially if they are family members or close friends to the deceased. Acknowledge everyone's grief and be kind and supportive to each other. Be ready to acknowledge that different people may want different things. For example, some may still want to set up and decorate a Christmas tree while others can't handle that in the absence of a loved spouse, parent or child who always had a special role in such things in the past. In such a situation, let the family get together, share their likes and dislikes with each other and come up with a close consensus that suits everyone as best as possible. It may be setting up the tree in a different room or in a different way. The main idea is to be sensitive to each other's feelings in this journey of grief so that you can all continue together as best as possible.

Thee is only one person who can take care of you better than any one else, and that is you. Your time of loss can also be a time of self discovery where you become aware of some strength you never knew existed within you. Talk about your loss and the pain that goes with the missing of your loved one. Find an effective way of gradually sharing your innermost memories or even writing letters to the departed loved ones. Go easy on yourself as you deal with the past regrets of the "if only'" and: should have's". Accept you did your best at the time. If need be, forgive yourself and move on. Some people come up with a collection of photographs of the deceased from their youth, their career, and their journeys in life until the latter years before they passed away. Traveling down the memory lane, visiting some interesting places with them in the mind and enjoying those spots and crossroads, might help ease their absence from your life. As often as you need to, find a quiet time and place. Jesus did that with his disciples (Mark 6:31). "Let's get away from the crowds for a while and rest". He invites you to go to a quiet and remote place him, where He will nurture you and speak to your emotional needs like no one else can. As you meditate on His words of comfort, allow him to touch, encourage and heal your grief. Remember too that just like a physical injury, healing from grief takes time. So let your grief unfold in its own way and its own time.

As time goes by, it will be helpful to search out for a grief support group near you. It is necessary and advisable to avoid isolating yourself as this will keep you from making the best out of life. It may either be in your church or an institution that helps gather people in the same journey to interact, encourage each other and share their own experiences. It will help decrease feelings of isolation and loneliness that go with grief and loss. It will be helpful to hear people share their coping strategies, the healing process and bring the companionship of others to your life. You get to talk and listen to people who understand the language of pain, those who out of their own personal tragedy can appreciate your confusion, your anger, your fluctuation in and out of sadness and joy without condemning you. You will meet grieving companions who will be able to just sit with you quietly and give you appropriate words when necessary. They will be better equipped to compassionately challenge you to move on without undue fear of hurting you as they know such a time must come through your own personal encounter with grief and sorrow. Find a group that is dealing with your own kind of grief if possible, e.g. the loss of a child, the loss of a spouse, surviving the loss of a loved one through suicide, etc.

It will also be helpful to look for appropriate reading material and books relevant to what you are dealing with. A visit to any of the major Christian stores will be a good place to begin with as the associates will give you suggestions on what they have. Other general bookstores will also have them in different categories. This will be a good way of spending your quiet time alone when you do not want to be in a crowd. Your bible is still the best book and some study bibles will give you relevant reading portions on the topic of grief and loss. Some will even illustrate experiences of old biblical figures like Job who experienced great tragedies and how they eventually recovered and were immeasurably blessed by God. Reading will help you realize that you are not alone and that if God has sustained and gradually healed others in their grief he will do the same for you too.

Mourning the death of different people brings different kinds of grief, e.g. the death of a child, a spouse, the death of a loved one suddenly in an accident of one kind or another or when one commits suicide. One might experience sudden outbursts of anger, frustrations, disappointment, depression, sleeplessness or oversleeping. In an attempt to help you, people who have not experienced grief and loss might erroneously cause you more pain than help without knowing it. In suicidal deaths, the deceased is often labeled or judged by people who have no clue what might have led them to commit suicide. If you are mourning for such a loss, perhaps you know what caused it, you may be angry at them but don't want anyone else to talk ill or negatively about them. Letting go and saying our good byes is the hardest thing. But it is harder still when we refuse to do so because it may linger on for too long and become complicated grief.

It is hard to expect ever recovering from grief. The best that might ever happen is that with time, we might cope better with our loss and feel the pain less often or with less intensity. We may gradually accept the reality that our loved one is really gone out of our lives. Even when we loose our elderly parents, there may still be feelings of abandonment or wondering if there is anything we could have done different for them. My parents, who both passed away three years ago with only three months in between them, are still very much in my mind constantly. More so my mother who was my best friend and prayer partner even though we lived in different continents towards their last few years of life. They were the best parents I could have prayed for and so their deaths brought a very deep sense of sorrow and grief that I thought would never cease to hurt. While I cannot forget their absence from my life, I am gradually getting to a point where I focus more on their achievements and impact on my life. Thus their memories and the legacies they left for us to continue working on have become a very integral part of our life's journey. I still struggle with the fact that I can no longer call my mother on the phone to express my concerns or even celebrate my big or small achievements in life. Harder still is the fact that I was never able to go home to bury my brother, my father or my mother.

These are some of the things that complicate the grieving and healing process for many people who for one reason or another were not able to do some closure to their losses. For many of us as Christians, our only comfort comes from knowing that God willing, we shall see our loved ones again, in a new life and place where there will be no good byes or grief. In the meantime, our dearly departed will remain in our hearts and lives through their memories and lives we shared in the past. These good memories of joyful times, funny incidents and family celebrations will support us in our remaining journeys. They will help us function better in our lives; especially remembering that we too have a destiny with death someday in the unknown future, when those that survive us will mourn and grieve for us. This is the reality of the cycle of life from generation to generation. The most important ingredients for our healing will be hope and courage in the future. The end of grief is not the end of memory, but the end of memory with great pain. However, the resolution to grief will involve selecting appropriate images and ways to remember the loved one who passed away. A person who touched our lives always remains a part of that life.

As time passes, and we get a better grip of life without those that have left this life, we are able to make some new choices without feeling guilty. Some people learn new things that help them through their grief and new growth. For one whose husband has managed everything to do with family finances etc, or where the wife planned all family activities, there will be lots of adjustments and learning new ways of continuing with our lives. Life opens up new realities and opportunities both in belief and priorities. Love takes a new meaning. Grief changes us but as much as possible should not be allowed to destroy us. However, losses propel us into a new life and we have to make deliberate choices on what lessons or memories we can carry on with us from our past into our new lives minus our dear departed loved ones. There will be need to let go of some things and learn new ways of handling life.

For those around a grieving person or family, there is a great deal we can do to help them cope with and heal their grief and loss. To a grieving/sorrowing person, little acts of kindness, words of encouragement and support of any kind, feel like a hug from God during their lonely desperate moments. In such times of sorrow and loss, it is the loss of a loved one to death, divorce, loss of good health or sanity of one's mind, the hug of a truly caring friend, even in silence, but with a caring eye contact, become like pillows for the hurts of a broken or wounded spirit. They encourage the grieving person endure their pain, sustain them until the cloud eases, passes or becomes bearable enough for them to continue their journey again. At times, it is just being present even when you do not know what to say, supporting them while they quietly process their thoughts and feelings as they come to terms with their loss. It is a cup of coffee or a glass of water, offering a wet wash cloth to cool off or clean their faces in weeping or just being a shoulder to lean on. Bringing a hot meal and encouraging them to eat something, inquiring if there is anything you can get for them from the grocery shop or even from another room, are some of the things they will remember for years to come as they reflect on how helpless and lost they had felt through their grief.

In grieving the loss of a loved one, wasted moments in all our lives, regrets for things that we had planned to do together but never got to do, become even more precious now that they can never be accomplished or repeated. At times they cause us to be more intentional with ensuring that what needs to be done is done or said before it is too late. When we grieve, it feels more like dying than growing. But as God wraps His loving arms around us, we have the assurance of His faithful care. It is important not to suppress one's grief and negative emotions because unless dealt with promptly, they will eventually catch up with you emotionally, physically or psychologically in the most unexpected moments or places.

In anticipatory grief, perhaps as one is battling cancer, AIDS, major heart ailments etc, the terminally ill person will be worried about many things that may go wrong for his/her family once they die. If they have children, they worry as to how they will make it in life as orphans or with a single parent. This is worse when the children are still very young, but even parents of adult children who can care for themselves, will still worry. The presence of a caring/compassionate friend or family, whom they have known and trusted for a long time, will be a great comfort and support.

As with getting help from friends and family, it is wise to be open to other forms of support. While your family wants to help you, their pain may be so great they cannot be of great or meaningful help. It may also be that their pain is too intense, their loss too threatening that they feel inadequate for you. On top of grief support groups, it may be necessary to seek professional counseling. Counseling is short-term assistance that helps us in confronting problematic challenges. It is the push, or lift that gets you over the hump. Seeking counseling demonstrates progress in one's grief and a willingness to do whatever it takes to find life beyond one's loss. This will provide the necessary continued reassurance that whatever you are experiencing is normal. The counselor will facilitate for you to verbalize and discuss your feelings. This may be very important if your emotions and feelings are too intense or painful to share with your family or close friends.

Counseling is particularly recommended in complicated grief, where suicidal thoughts or a desire to hurt one-self or others is evident. If alcohol and drugs are also mixed with the grieving process, counseling may be an urgent necessity to protect the grieving person from angry self-destruction. The same challenge or sorrow and pain faces a healthy athletic ballerina dancer or actor who suddenly becomes a paraplegic after a motor accident. The family deeply mourns the loss of a normal life, shattered/broken dreams for their loved one almost as much as a death. With a deep sense of loss, the family life changes for ever as they must now completely arrange and reorganize themselves for a whole new journey of caring for this one who for a long time may be totally dependent on them. She or he will have moments of great anger, frustrations and hopelessness as they grieve their own personal losses. She/he may not want to live anymore and their caring family has to climb up all these mountains, cross all the rivers of pain and sorrow, or at times just sit on the ashes of his/her healthy, active and athletic past that has been cruelly and permanently snatched away in a twinkling of an eye in a freak accident.

The friend or family, who intentionally chooses to remain closely connected with the wounded paraplegic even when they are angry and shouting or cursing, through their moments of depression, shows their love and care in action at a very high emotional, physical or spiritual cost. It speaks a million words of encouragement to this grieving person telling them they are still valued and cherished despite their losses. Assuring them that as much as God helps, the family will not abandon them. This may eventually be the motivation that gives them reason and strength to fight for survival.

As we all struggle to process all kinds of grief and losses, May the good Lord grant us a positive outcome after our sorrow, where we long to obey and hunger for his word as the only lasting solution to our irreparable losses. Some one said this in their grief, "*I have been through the valley of weeping, the valley of pain and sorrow. But God of all comfort was with me, at hand to uphold and sustain me*". Hold on to your HOPE in God who will help you survive. No matter how tough life may get, you can and will pull through. Eventually you will be able to say "*I am confident I will see my beloved again*".

As you slowly journey on, one step/one day at a time, do not put limits on yourself. Your dreams are waiting to be realized. This may even be what your departed loved one would really wish for you – to achieve the goals that the two of you might have planned for. Do not leave your important decisions to chance. As best as the Lords helps you, "*Reach for your peak, your goal and your Prize*". Remember too that "The old unhealed wounds of grief will linger, influence all aspects of your life, your living and particularly your loving. Grief work and active mourning is the very pathway through which you reconcile your losses. The opposite of befriending your life losses is to try to control them.

Underneath the impulse to control is fear that you will have to experience feelings and helplessness and hurt". (Alan D. Wolfelt, Ph.D.)

Surrendering to your grief paradoxically ushers you in the capacity to live life with a sense of purpose and creative energy. There is life beyond loss. It will be a changed life with a hope that as time passes, the grieving person will feel better to find new joy and peace again as they strive to live beyond the loss.

13

Handling the Holidays

Holidays are very tough and tend to magnify one's loss and grief. They bring sadness, loneliness, anger, anxiety, nightmares and lack of interest in any activities. This is tough when you anticipate a season of celebration of one kind or another knowing your departed loved one will never be there again to do the things you always did with them in the past. Reactions to the first anniversary may be very intense but one is bound to feel better gradually. You may still suddenly break down and weep unexpectedly and that too is normal. Again, be fair with yourself and remind yourself and others that your special relationship with the deceased, now gone for ever, was unique to you and only you know the real depth of your loss and grief. This is especially profound in the death of a spouse and a lifetime companion. Feel free to handle the season in whichever way makes you comfortable and causes you less pressure and grief. Some people choose to forego certain activities that were shared in the past; others avoid visiting places they went together etc. A few other people may choose to do the opposite and replicate their mode of past celebrations, even leaving the chair that the deceased liked nearby but empty, and talk about the deceased as if they are participating in the events. Whichever way it is done, as long as it does not add any more sorrow and is okay with the grieving person, it is okay. Whatever you do in celebrating any anniversaries or holidays from this time on, do it in a way that is comfortable and enjoyable for you personally and not necessarily how others feel you should. After all, you are the one experiencing the depth and reality of the absence of your loved one who is no longer there to share these moments and events with you.

14

THE SERIOUS IMPACT OF CHRONIC PAIN

Definition of Pain:

Scientists define pain as

-*".....an unpleasant sensory and emotional experience associated with actual or potential tissue damage, or described in terms of such damage." (IASP 1992 – International Association for Study of Pain)*

An uncomfortable sensation that bothers or upsets the person.

Pain is whatever the person says it is, occurring whenever the person says it Hurts (Margo McCaffrey, RN.MS, FAAN)

As we continue to focus attention on the things that bring us grief at different crossroads of life, I feel it is necessary and very important to highlight the constant challenges that go hand in hand with chronic pain, regardless of our age, gender, economic status, nationality or religious beliefs. Unfortunately, we do not give enough attention to this topic., and when we do, it is often and sadly too late. The truth is that pain of any kind in any part of our body is a tell-tale sign of something going out of the norm in our system for one reason or another. It may come to sensitize us or draw our attention to some organ in our body that has been invaded by viruses or bacteria or by some other foreign body causing us to malfunction.

One good example is the strong pain that go alongside different kinds of cancer, heart diseases, etc. Many a times, people put up with great pains for long periods of time, all in the effort of appearing bold and strong even when they are groaning and broken on the inside. This is a well known trend in many cultures of the world where expressing pain is seen as a weakness. It is not unheard of to learn that someone has lost their lives trying to endure terrible pains without seeking help until they could bear it no more. This has caused many regrets in many families mourning the loss of a child, a parent, a spouse or a close friend. How many times have we heard people say that "I wish I had paid more attention when I saw so and so begin to change and deteriorate for the worse". We all can perhaps think of some women somewhere in our communities who lost their lives and at times their unborn babies as one thing led to another during labor resulting in complications needing greater attention. They died trying very hard to look bold and endure the pangs of natural birth, without realizing that they had some complications and they needed to admit their pains were beyond endurance so the cause could be addressed. On the part of the healthcare professionals, there have been times when they thought these ladies were just fearful of labor pains, thus gave them a little more time until it was too late. This is more critical under community and village mid-wives who have little or no professional training for their work.

It has been my worst experience and I believe worse still for families, to hear a surgeon inform the patient and their family that when they operated on them, they found out that the cancer, or whatever else they were suffering from, had advanced too much beyond control and there was nothing much they could do to extend their lives. I have been called to accompany a doctor many times and comfort the family as they receive such news. Many times you will hear the sad regrets and people wishing they had encouraged their loved ones to seek a doctors help as soon as they started getting sick. Cancer is one of the best examples because in some cases it explodes and advances into different parts of the body after a certain stage where no chemotherapy or radiation can contain it any longer and the doctors have the responsibility of telling the patient and the families that the patient has just a certain length of time before finally dying from it. This must be some of the most devastating news for any family. Shock, denial and disbelief quickly set in the impact of the news do not just affect the patient but the entire family. Many lives have been totally and seriously changed for ever, by a situation that could at times could have been avoided or diverted had someone been more alert and observant of the changes and advances of the cancer.

Despite the fact that the loved ones would still end up dying from the disease, I would still apply what we tell HIV|AIDS victims, their families and those living and interacting with them – even when you know they are dying, help them as much as you can and strive to put life in their days instead of putting days into their lives. I am talking about giving them quality life and relationship into every day that you still have with them instead of wishfully hoping for more days that may no longer be there.

When you seriously consider the impact of chronic pain on the sufferer and their family as well as caregivers if any, you will find that it will not only affect them physically but also economically, socially, spiritually, morally, in their relationships etc, etc. There is great grief resulting from the fact the chronic pain victim is derailed in many ways from their normal life style and company because they cannot comfortably participate in some activities, depending on what is ailing them. Consider those affected in the back, legs, shoulders, neck, etc whose mobility may gradually be limited and eventually some becoming paralyzed and wheelchair bound. Their chronic pain is definitely going to affect them in all the above ways and life totally changed. With chronic pain comes loneliness and isolation which may eventually lead to depression and mood swings which unless treated can affect everyone around the patient whether at home or place of work.

Unfortunately chronic pain is no respecter of age and it has been known to cripple both the young and the old. It is important that we pay attention when our children complain of aches and pains that cannot be properly explained or understood. Gone are the days when we simply ignored them, telling them that "those are growing pains". I am sure many of us have experienced the death of young children from cancer, heart ailments etc. either in our families, among our friends or in the wider communities around us. This should then sensitize us to the fact that children too may have chronic pains like the old people. It is only fair that they too should receive optimal treatment and pain medication for their relief as they too deserve just as much as their parents or grand-parents. Otherwise we will suffer from regrets that could be avoided and possibly lives saved as necessary.

Marital relationships are not exempted from the effects of chronic pain. It will take immense understanding from both husband and wives, if one of them has chronic pain affecting or limiting their intimacy one way or the other. It takes a lot of love and patience with each other to save their marriage. I am living witness that chronic pain can easily reverse the roles between parents and their children. Having lived with a chronic back pain for over 37 years before I yielded to a major back surgery only because paralysis was creeping in, I found myself depending first on the nurses in the hospital to help me with bathing and toilet needs. Inevitably when I went home

I had to depend on my children for the same needs. For any parent this takes a lot of yielding because you are left with no choice. For everyone under such circumstances, it takes your pride and control over your life away and quickly humbles you down whether you like it or not. For the children, it is also a very hard and humbling thing to wake up one day and see the mother or father who has always been your pillar or strength looking up to you for simple things like feeding, brushing their hair, climbing in and out of bed, going to the toilet and even bathing. This has been your hero who taught you to bathe, clean house, ride a bike and perhaps even drive your first car, cheered you to climb the heights of life who now depends on you for their lives as a result of chronic pain. How then shall we not want to do anything to help them control and manage their pains and address the cause before they go this far into being partially or totally disabled?? It does not matter how young or old one is, but one can very quickly be pushed into the serious role of the family bread winner when the parents and original bread winners are gradually or suddenly grounded by chronic pain for various reasons, know or sometimes unknown.

Pain relief is a basic right and these are some of the things to be expected:

- Pain relief is a basic healthcare right
- People seeking healthcare with pain expect:
    - To be asked about their pain
    - To have their reports of pain believed
    - To have pain prevented and relieved whenever possible
- Talk with the healthcare team about:
    - finding the cause of pain (if unknown)

- Treatment options – including referral to a pain management doctor
- Ways of reducing your pain to a comfortable level
- Improving function

Complete relief may not always be possible, but every effort is worth it all.

Working as a volunteer with the American Pain Foundation is one of the best things that ever happened to me. It is for this reason that I finally acknowledge my back pain after many years of enduring and playing it down. Like everyone else, through many stages of my life including having my youngest two children, I acted bold and endured untold pain, but doing everything to appear bold and strong in the eyes of the beholder, even though it caused me intermittent semi paralysis on my right side for years and years. I was told many times that this is normal especially in the child bearing age and thereafter. Different doctors kept telling me to bear it as there was nothing they could do and gave me pain medications sparingly. I am sure I speak for many people under the similar circumstances. With all due respect, men rarely talk about their pain and so are prone to finding out the underlying causes, years later that they might have saved their lives great pains had they admitted it and sought help. The deeper I got involved as a chronic pain advocate in the Power over Pain Action Network with this important organization, the more bold I became and gave myself and others permission to acknowledge their pain before it was too late.

The main focus of the American Pain Foundation's advocacy efforts which I consider very vital is to inform, motivate and harness the millions of voices of people affected by pain, in order to raise public awareness and promote the best pain policy and practice. The under-treatment of pain is based on many factors, including under reporting by people experiencing pain, lack of responsiveness of the medical system, lack of healthcare professional training, regulatory barriers and access to care. We need to encourage people to speak to their healthcare providers about their pain, show where it hurts, say what makes it better or worse and be able to explain to their doctors whatever concerns or worries they have regarding their pain. It is critical that everyone receives optimal care and access is not denied. Drug abuse is a serious problem in our country, but addressing the drug abuse must not be at the cost of limiting access to pain medications for legitimate needs of pain relief

Prompt treatment is very important and has the potential to alleviate many problems. Under-treated pain has tremendous negative impact on individual families, communities, the workforce, healthcare systems and our overall economy. The annual cost of chronic pain in the United States, including healthcare expenses, lost income and productivity, is estimated to be $100 billion (2) (see APF website for reference – http//www.painfoundation.org/newsroom/reporter-resources/pain-facts-figures.htm) Other barriers to better pain management that need to be eliminated which include

- Communication problems between patients and the medical personnel. Patients assuming that others should know and understand that they have pain.

- Fear of pain's meaning and treatment. Fear by patients of being judged and listed as drug seekers and therefore not seeking prompt treatment.

- Professional response – Doctors fear of regulatory scrutiny, inadequate pain management training and lack of awareness of the necessity for quick and effective response to reports of pain.

According to the National Center for Health Statistics in the USA in 2006 with Chart book on Trends in the Health of Americans (Hyatsville, MD: 68-71), the Scope of Pain was as follows:

- Over 76.5 Americans suffered with pain
- This meant that 4 out of 10 Americans were suffering with pain.
- 1 out of 19 with acute pain
- 3 out of 10 with chronic pain.

Acute Pain: This ranges from mild to severe; usually signals injury of a body part. Pain is temporary and typically goes away when the injury or illness is treated.

Chronic Pain: This ranges from mild to severe; persistent pain, lasting months to years, causes not always known; may be disease-related; often requires complex treatments.

The Good News is – Relief is often possible

- Early Treatment can cut the lasting problems caused by pain that affect the mind, body and the spirit
- There are effective methods of reducing pain, and restoring lost joy, functioning and quality of life.
- There are pain specialists that can help treat your pain.
- EVERYONE is different and responds differently to pain.

"No prescription is more valuable than knowledge (C. Everett Koop, MD

Appendix

Personal Stories Shared:
_____

a) _Rosalind Zeigler, BBA, MSM_

I have had the pleasure of reading *"Healing Hope for Your Grief & Bereavement"* by Dr. penny . I am exceedingly impressed with the wide range of issues related to grief, such as the importance of wills – that are discussed and explored throughout the book. This book can be used as educational resource in institutions of learning, or as a personal tool, to help individuals understand how to grieve appropriately and in a healthy way, at their own pace as best as possible.

There is unquestionably a great market and need for this book because every person will undoubtedly lose a loved one which will cause them to experience grief and bereavement many times throughout their lifetime. This book is therefore a treasure because it is different from most books that I have read or have knowledge of on the topic of grief. It is inclusively written and designed to cater for different kinds of losses that include the loss of a child, a spouse, a parent, marital relationships through divorce and separation, etc. She addresses the grief that comes from losing a job, losing a home through foreclosure, the impact of terminal illnesses etc. It is filled with Dr. Penny's personal stories as she walked with others in their journey. It is a wise investment that can provide ongoing guidance during turbulent times on multiple occasions.

What I like about this book is that it is Bible based, using scripture as a guide to help those grieving to remember God's promise, "*I am with you always*". Dr. Penny uses her personal life experiences as a Chaplain, a sister, a daughter, and a friend, who has had to travel the difficult road of experiencing grief personally. She shares her experiences with the dying. I could feel her love shining from the words on the paper as she compassionately held hands, praying with those taking their last breath. Dr. Penny offers her professional advice that comes from wisdom, experience and education to bring hope to the hopeless.

Lastly, as I was nearing the completion of the manuscript, I was taken back by what I was reading. Tears ran down my face making it impossible to ready any further. I took a break from reading and did not finish until weeks later. Dr. Penny shared a story about a how a young man and a friend of hers, had dealt with cancer from his early teens into young adulthood. She explains how he dealt with shame and embarrassment of being ridiculed by schoolmates, because years of chemotherapy and radiation coupled with multiple surgeries left his physical appearance different and unique from others of his age. How he would be forced to remove his cap in public places by adults who were often rude and showed no compassion. How he suffered from low self esteem even though he had nothing to be ashamed of because he had beaten the odds, and was a three times cancer survivor. Dr. Penny highlights that there is a great need for people to understand how to deal compassionately and caringly with teenagers and young adults who are grieving for not being able to experience life as a normal kid, and who forced to deal with mortality when they should actually be enjoying their youth.

The young man that Dr. Penny is referring to is my son. I had no idea that his story would ever become part of such a powerful tool, so passionately written and intended to help thousands of people understand the impact of grief and bereavement and how best to support those experiencing it. This personal story, like many others shared in this book has touched my soul in a very special way. It makes me realize just how important this book is to the world of today, where life has become so challenging and people have to battle grief and bereavement constantly. I am left with a greater understanding of my personal grief as I continue to heal as a parent who has experienced grief for the physical, emotional and spiritual pain her son has and continues to endure. The pain of grief is not severe today as it was at the beginning of this journey. However, it silently lingers on for lack of proper understanding of grief and bereavement in the world. The adverse effect of this is that we therefore lack the appropriate support and care that Dr. Penny is portraying in her book. Her knowledge and commitment to share and educate people on how to support others through these experiences is very timely, clearly written and presented as *A MUST READ RESOURCE BOOK. I know for sure that God is with me.*

b) *Mary Mathangani, RN*

As a registered nurse with many years experience, I have experienced both personally at the loss of members of my family and friends as well as through my profession. It was therefore such an encouraging thing when Dr. Penny invited me to share my own experience in something that we would all rather never experience. Unfortunately, the truth is that if one has not yet experienced grief by now, a day is coming when it will surely knock at your door and you will have to deal with it. I was moved and challenged by the title of this book *"Healing Hope For Your Grief And Bereavement"* which is not only eye catching but also speaks a great message in a world where *"Hope"* seems like a lost dream for many. Dr. Penny, a humble, intelligent, articulate, enthusiastic servant of God as a minister of the Gospel is well known for her compassion and care for others in need. She encourages and motivates others to look beyond whatever is challenging them and hope for better things ahead.

I have known Dr. Penny for more than 10 years as one who is totally committed to her ministry of caring for those struggling with grief and bereavement, not just because of losing a loved one to death. Dr. Penny also caters for those broken by terminal illnesses, divorce and separation, loss of jobs, loss of homes to foreclosures, bankruptcy, challenges of advancing age and poor health and so many other things that often make life unbearable. I have known her to give and care for others unselfishly and sacrificing herself in her work beyond every measure.

Many times when I have encountered a challenging situation in my place of work with patients and families struggling with the grief of eminent death, I have often been drawn to calling for her guidance and advice on how best to handle such situations. This is because I have always found her readily equipped with the appropriate words and actions at such times and very confident in how she handles the challenging moments. Dr. Penny has mentored me and many others in my profession and been a great resource in our communities. Dr. Penny helps you to explore all the possibilities and horizons that can be used for different occasions. Above all, she is a God fearing woman of great faith who works with Godly principles and guidance in all that she does both privately, publicly and professionally. All the examples she has shared in this book are true both from her personal life and those that she experiences as she ministers or counsels those experiencing grief and bereavement for one reason or another.

One thing I admire about Dr. Penny is that she is a good and patient listener who pays attention to what you have to say before she speaks. When she speaks, she does so with wisdom and carefully chosen words that end up nurturing, soothing and comforting your pain, heartache and brokenness. She is very reassuring in her counseling and empowers people to look up into the future with **HOPE** even when things are very tough. While Dr. Penny has been a great resource for me professionally, I have been blessed with her grief support many times when my family has experienced the painful loss of a loved one. Dr. Penny has been known to be there for the grieving families in our community not only emotionally but also physically and in whichever other ways her help was needed. She has proved herself a trusted and dependable friend in times of crises for many and is highly respected and cherished for that. For all the many times Dr. Penny has counseled us through such moments, I cannot remember anything she ever said that I wish she had not uttered.

From a professional perspective, Dr. Penny shares a lot of important information on how best to minister and care not only for the dying patient both at home or in the hospital environment but also for the families and friends who are dealing with anticipatory grief. She has addressed different forms of grief that is encountered by people of all ages where none of us is exempted. Dr. Penny sensitizes us to be careful what we say to each other during moments of crises, reminding us that great damage is done that can never be totally repaired and bad memories created in moments of grief even when it is not intentionally done. She makes us comfortable with the fact that we can be of great support to the grieving families just by our silent presence and that we do not necessarily have to say anything which at times ends up more damaging than the silent presence.

One of the greatest gifts and empowerment that Dr. Penny has given me is the fact that it is okay to weep with the patients and families if we are that much touched by their heartache, just as Jesus wept at the death of Lazarus. All along I felt I needed to remain strong, almost to the point of having no emotions while it is healthy and appropriate to connect with others emotionally in their pain and loss.

As I remember many instances when I have felt helpless and ill equipped to support those mourning and grieving, I wish many times that Dr. Penny's book and words of wisdom had been there for me then. I would therefore recommend this book as *"A MUST READ BOOK "* for everyone, and especially in the healthcare profession. The reality is that we will all encounter grief and bereavement somewhere along the path of life whether young or old because no one is exempted. This book is also ideal for church ministry, Sunday school classes, bible study groups, support groups etc. Dr. Penny has something fro everyone. I thank God for the way He is using her to share such powerful and important information as a resource for different challenges.

c) *Margaret Howard Barrow, MSW, Licensed Certified Social Worker*

As I read through Dr. Penny's manuscript *"Healing Hope For Your Grief & Bereavement"* I imagined how people would quickly wonder what is so new in this book that one has not already heard or read in other books. My immediate answer would be that you will either learn new things or gain deeper understanding of what you know and probably benefit both ways.

But as I read her book, I was vividly reminded of my own journey of grief at the death of my dear mother a short while ago. I thanked God that through our friendship and professional companionship, I was greatly blessed by Dr. Penny's grief and bereavement ministry in our hospital where she leads and facilitates several support groups. I have had the pleasure of attending several of them and experienced her compassion and nurturing presence for those that are experiencing the painful pangs of loss and wondering whether the pain will ever subside.

I can attest to Dr. Penny's comforting and assuring words of God's unfailing love and faithful presence at all times under all circumstances. This is Dr. Penny's bedrock and her only source of strength. She will tell you that very quickly. that in her humility lies her unique ability to bring the broken-hearted to Jesus rather than take credit for the healing He brings in moments of crises, sorrow and brokenness.

Dr. Penny's immense wisdom and compassionate care comes from many years of ministry in different cultures. Her teaching and counsel are rooted in her experience with God in serving the sufferers in hospitals, hospices, villages and cities of both worlds developed and developing. Dr. Penny has a deep familiarity with the workings of the human heart both in joy and sorrow. Her own personal experiences bring a unique richness in her ministry to the broken hearted because she ministers from her heart with deep understanding and compassion. Dr. Penny has been pierced with more grief than most of us will ever know. Yet she has chosen a different path from most others in the valley. We mostly tend to seek quiet and rest as we walk in sorrow and healing under God. Dr. Penny chooses to obey God's call to go to those being pierced and those that we would rather avoid as was done by many in the parable of *The Good Samaritan*. She risks the pain of remembered agony from her own journey. She is constantly trusting God (and encouraging others to do so) to bring her through that pain of grief or bereavement whenever it strikes as it often will. She encourages us all to trust God to provide our healing and rest.

Even though Dr. Penny has been there for me emotionally and morally while I grieved my mother's death, I feel and experience a deeper and genuine support as I read through her book. As a professional social worker and patient care representative in a big hospital, I am bound to encounter grieving families who are struggling with all kind of issues that accompany the death of a loved one. There are times when

I also have to deal with the grief that challenges families during a major illness of a loved one including finances, healthcare decisions and plans, loss of livelihoods, foreclosures as a result of major illnesses that consume family finances etc. I have found Dr. Penny's book to be a great resource, not only when grieving a death but all the other losses mentioned above. She offers numerous great ideas for personal and professional application in different crossroads of the journey of life.

After reading this powerful book which is not only well and clearly written, you will come out better equipped to help others left behind by their loved ones. You will have a source of solace when it is your time on that dark road. You will be empowered by having shared time with Dr. Penny and her ever present God through the valleys of loss and tears. I would highly recommend this book to each and everyone.

Finally, Letting Go

As weeks turn into months and months turn into a year, the grieving person begins to adjust to the absence of the loved one now gone beyond the grave for ever. There is no set period for this because like mentioned over and over throughout the previous chapters; each person grieves in a very individual manner. Yet, it is the very act of grief and mourning that facilitates the healing process. Letting go includes replacing the painful memories of one's loss with some positive pleasant feelings and memories. This process will only begin once we have gone over the various phases of grief and fully acknowledged the reality and depth of our grief.

Letting go of the pain and grief will take many trials and errors coupled with a lot of patience from the grieving person and those around them. It may be like taking two steps forward and one step backwards. And this too is normal with grieving. It will involve many changes in life; making new friends, changing some habits or activities and finding new ones that are appropriate to where the grieving person is in life. The moments of painful tears and anguish of the loss, anger and guilt will all be part of this process and must be dealt with realistically without being suppressed.

There will also be moments of going back and forth with questions like "why me", "why now" etc. Grief will at times feel like one is walking through some deep waters that are threatening to wash you away. As you strive to walk out of these waters of sorrow and grief, you will need to reach out to other people's hands for help in new relationships, renewing of old friendships etc in order to start experiencing healing from your grief. The grieving person, who is willing and finally able to start the process of letting go, will start picking up the broken pieces of their lives and reconstructing again. This way they will start moving on with life albeit with bits and pieces of the past life missing and being replaced with new additions.

At this point, support groups, pastoral care from your church and pastor, or help from professional counselors will go along way to facilitate in the process of letting go and rebuilding of lives impacted and broken by the grief and loss of one kind or another. This will be a major turning point where support goes a long way in nurturing and affirming the grieving person so as to propel them forward out of the pit of pain and self-pity that may sub-consciously be holding them from the path of healing. These support systems are not necessarily permanent, but temporary pillars to lean on until one is strong enough to function on their own. For some months or even years, one may feel the need to be in and out of them. One must be made free to come and go as suits their healing process because they are the best judges of how well or badly they are doing with their grief. Letting go is getting into a partnership with God, choosing to yield to forces beyond ourselves and trusting God with ourselves through this path of pain sorrow and grief. It is to live in grace and full trust in God. It is hearing God's soft voice of assurance and comfort and daring to allow him to walk for us when we are too weak to walk, as in the poem of the "Footprints". Letting go is sweet victory over the fear of succumbing to the pain of loss and grief. It is looking forward into the future in full confidence that God will never leave you alone to drown in your sorrow and pain.

Scriptures on Encouragement & Grief Recovery

A few of these scriptures have been mentioned in the document but others are not.

1. Isaiah 43:1-5
2. John 11:25-26
3. 2 Corinthians 5:8
4. Jeremiah 1:5
5. Philippians 4:14
6. 1 Thessalonians 4:13-14
7. Psalm 143:4
8. Psalm 23:4
9. John 11:35
10. Mark 6:31
11. John 14:27
12. Philippians 4:7
13. Ephesians 3:16
14. Psalm 18:2
15. Psalm 147:3
16. Ephesians 2:14
17. Isaiah 26:3
18. Luke 4:18-19

19. Jeremiah 6:14
20. Isaiah 43:4b
21. Deuteronomy 33:27
22. 2 Kings 20:5b
23. Psalm 34:18
24. Psalm 126:5
25. Isaiah 43:1b
26. Isaiah 49:15
27. Mathew 5:4
28. Revelations 21:2-8

Works Cited:

1. The Holy Bible – New Living Translation
2. Ira Byrock – 1998
3. Russell Friedman & John W. James of the Grief Recovery Institute 2002-2006
4. Dr. Elizabeth Kubler-Ross
5. Stephen Levine
6. Washington Irving
7. Dr. Alan D. Wolfelt
8. Oscar Romero
9. Kahil Gibran
10. Margo McCaffrey, RN, MS, FAAN
11. American Pain Foundation
12. National Center For Health Statistics In The USA – 2006
13. Hyattsville, MD
14. C. Everett Koop, MD

TO GOD BE ALL HONOR AND GLORY, FOR GUIDING ME THOUGH THIS WORK AND FOR ALL THOSE THAT IT WILL TOUCH, ENCOURAGE, COMFORT, SUPPORT AND GUIDE IN THE JOURNEY OF HEALING THEIR GRIEF.